Thing Feigned or Imagined

THE CRAFT IN FICTION

The Craft
in Fiction

*Thing Feigned
or Imagined*

FRED STENSON

THE BANFF CENTRE
PRESS

The publishers and authors have generously given
permission to reprint the following copyrighted works.
"The Dog in the Van," from *White Buick*, by Greg
Hollingshead. Copyright © 1992 by Greg Hollingshead.
Reprinted with permission by Oolichan Books.
"Visitation," from *Mona Lisa Smiled a Little*, by Rachel
Wyatt. Copyright © 1999 by Rachel Wyatt. Reprinted
with permission by Oolichan Books. "Half-Past Eight,"
from *A Sleep Full of Dreams*, by Edna Alford. Copyright ©
1981 by Edna Alford. Reprinted with permission by
Oolichan Books. "Stranger than Fiction," copyright ©
Diane Schoemperlen 1989, currently in her collection of
selected stories, *Red Plaid Shirt* (Harper Collins 2002).
"Positive Images," from *Working Without a Laugh Track*, by
Fred Stenson. Copyright © 1990 by Fred Stenson.
Reprinted with permission by Coteau Books.

NATIONAL LIBRARY OF CANADA
CATALOGUING IN PUBLICATION DATA

Stenson, Fred, 1951–
    Thing feigned or imagined

    ISBN 978-0-92015-993-4

    1. Fiction—Technique. 2. Fiction—Authorship.
I. Title.
PN3355.S73 2002   808.3   C2002-910787-3

Copy edited by: Maureen Nicholson
Cover and book design: Alan Brownoff
First Impression printed and bound in Canada by:
Kromar Printing Ltd., 2002
Second Impression printed and bound in Canada by:
Marquis Printing, 2015
Cover photograph by: Richard Siemens

The Banff Centre Press gratefully acknowledges the
Canada Council for the Arts for its support of our
publishing program.

BANFF CENTRE PRESS
Box 1020–107 Tunnel Mountain Drive
Banff, Alberta T1L 1H5
www.banffcentrepress.ca

fiction /1. A thing feigned or imaginatively invented.
(OXFORD ENGLISH DICTIONARY)

Contents

Introduction

This book is a practical guide to the craft of fiction.

Now in my thirtieth year of writing, I have never in all that time been an instructor or professor, not in the sense of teaching regular courses and assigning grades. What I have been is a mentor to many writers in non-academic settings. I have taught evening non-credit courses in fiction (a couple of them in Canadian federal penitentiaries). I have been a writer-in-residence at libraries and colleges. I have led many one- or two-day workshops. Most recently, I have edited fiction at several Banff Centre writing studios. Since 2001, I have directed Banff's Wired Writing Studio, an experiment in providing mentorship and community on-line.

One of the striking things about working with writers is how much of the craft they do by instinct. This is a good thing in the initial act of fictional creation, but leads to trouble in the editing phase. Often, good as the writers are, they don't understand what they have done, or what its effect is, moment by moment, on readers. This too would be fine if the fiction they had created was perfect. If not, they do not always know how to make it better. Unable to improve the story or novel, they often abandon it as a failure and move on, hoping to write a better work next time.

This is a wasteful practice, wasteful of time and talent. The fiction they have thrown away may not be a failure at all but a success in waiting. What it waits for is improvement, and given a better understanding of how fiction works, those writers could work their so-called failures into more pleasing and effective forms.

Often the mentoring process is about showing writers where improving change can occur. I point out where the writing isn't working, isn't having the desired effect, or is having an unexpected bad effect on readers. The writer and I, or the writer alone, then conceive a solution. When writers learn from experience or mentoring how to find and fix the problems in their work, they become self-sufficient, complete.

This book is not about methods of inspiration for writers or the philosophy of writing—and not because they aren't important. Many excellent books already exist for purposes of opening the wellsprings of a writer's creativity. If that's what you're looking for, it exists elsewhere. What this book does instead is provide practical help for diagnosing problems of fictional mechanism and craft: it's a combination of instruction and troubleshooting.

At the end of each chapter are exercises called "Your Process." The chapters and exercises are steps in a self-guided process to help you complete one or more short stories. The chapters move you through a process of thinking about fiction and doing fiction, from the search for a fiction-worthy idea, through to editing and the consideration of publication. The book is designed to be helpful to the beginner, but not so basic as to be patronizing to that beginner or unhelpful to a more experienced writer.

The book also includes five short stories. Authors Rachel Wyatt, Edna Alford, Greg Hollingshead, and Diane Schoemperlen are among the best fiction writers in Canada, with demonstrated excellence in short fiction. Among them, they have two Canadian Governor General's Awards, a Marion Engel Award, and many other honours. The fifth story is my own. The stories are used in various ways to illustrate points of craft. They also provide the inspiration of good writing.

Not all the ideas in these pages will be original. Perhaps none of it is. Storytelling might be humankind's most ancient art, which suggests that the training of storytellers came soon after. What I can vouch for is that each piece of advice has been invented or chosen, then used as an answer to a writer's real dilemma—and has been found helpful. In other words, my advice is tested.

FRED STENSON

Fiction or Non-Fiction

WHATEVER THE DIFFERENCE IS,
IT ISN'T THE WORDS

I have listened to smart, well-educated people talk in circles, obsessively, even angrily, on the subject of the distinction between fiction and non-fiction. Some speak of the characteristics of fiction and the characteristics of non-fiction, and they invariably trap themselves in the fact that most of those characteristics (point of view, dialogue, scene-setting, story, information, fact, truth, lie) are not unique to fiction or non-fiction but are common to both.

Someone else in the room always gets furious over the need to distinguish. Who cares? Why be so fussy about categories? I suspect that if this person were to pick up a newspaper, read a story on the front page, and discover later it was entirely made up—a work of fiction—he or she might care a lot.

To show how most definitions of fiction crash and burn, let me produce one. Fiction is "an untrue story that is ultimately truthful." That has a nice ring.

Balanced. It explains the feeling we get when we are reading something so true to life that it is almost better than the day-to-day events around us. Lovely.

But what about fiction where the story *is* true? In a novel called *The Trade*, based on Canada's nineteenth-century fur trade, I drew many stories from the historical record and filled the blanks with stories I made up. Is *The Trade* less a work of fiction for having true stories in it? I don't think so.

So already, the definition has a problem. One big fictional category—fictional works based on real people and events—won't fit in it.

And who says a fictional story has to be ultimately truthful? Since the beginning of the oral tale (giants, gorgons, dragons) to the latest work of satire and fabulism, fiction is full of things that are ultimately untruthful. They have not happened on this planet. They probably *could* not. That fact is part of the charm of a certain kind of story.

This definition of fiction, like most of its kind (and perhaps like all), fails.

Non-fiction is just as hard to define. Many works of non-fiction have been proven to contain things totally made up by their authors. Does that transform them from non-fiction to fiction? Oddly enough, it does not. In a book of non-fiction, Annie Dillard produced the fact that her cat came through the window one night and kneaded on her nightdress with bloody paws. It wasn't her experience. It was someone else's. The entire world of American non-fiction seemed to tremble and rage for years over this breaking of the unwritten commandment of non-fiction that its contents be true. But at no time did Annie Dillard's book transform from non-fiction to fiction. In Canada, we've gone through the same cycle with the sometimes whimsical non-fictions of Farley Mowat.

I won't go on with other definitions to prove that you can pull the wings off all of them. Let's just assume you can, and move on.

Whether or not fiction and non-fiction can be defined in a way that holds them separate, I still contend that the difference is important—fundamental in fact—to the creation of either. And I believe there is a method for reliably distinguishing between them. It is not in the words or the arrangement of words, or their factuality or made-up-ness that the difference is located; *it is in what the text purports to be*. A novel purports to be a work of the imagination, so no matter how many reliable facts, figures, and events it contains, the work is still fiction. Non-fiction purports to be a work documenting a non-fictional, non-imaginary reality. Hence, when you pick up the *Midnight News* and read that a psychic's head has exploded or that a two-headed calf has won another spelling bee, what you are reading, though perhaps made-up, is non-fiction. Why? Because it *purports* to be non-fiction.

The ultimate proof that the difference between fiction and non-fiction is not in the words came in the 1980s when a writer published a book he claimed was a slightly edited version of a recently discovered authentic diary kept by a nineteenth-century Irishman named Gerald Keegan. Keegan, like thousands of Irish, had tried to escape the potato famine by ship to Canada. There was typhus aboard his "coffin ship," and though he survived the voyage, his ship was not allowed to land in the cities of Quebec. It went to the quarantine island of Grosse Isle in the St. Lawrence River. There, thousands of Irish men, women, and children—including Keegan—suffered and died. And now the Keegan diary had been discovered by the writer in a chance encounter with a Laval University academic. The implication when the book came out was that the Canadian government of the day tried to repress the book, to conceal the disservice the government had done to these unfortunate Irish immigrants.

Things got rolling in 1991 when an Irish publishing house picked up the book and released it as an authentic, famine-era, coffin-ship, quarantine-island diary. It shot to the top of the Irish bestseller list and stayed there for two years.

Then a couple of astute observers, an Irishman and a Canadian, acting independently, did some research and claimed the book was a hoax. The Keegan diary had hardly changed since it was written by Scottish Protestant writer and editor Robert Sellar in Quebec almost a century earlier. It was published as a novel, in Huntington, Quebec, in 1895, under the title *Summer of Sorrow*. This claim was eventually proven beyond doubt and accepted by all, to the considerable embarrassment of many.

I was among the embarrassed and for a not very good reason, given that the hoax had already been revealed before I read the diary. In the early 1990s, I was researching a television docudrama on Canadian immigration, and I came across the diary in an anthology of works by and about Irish Canadians. I read it. I wept. I was all for including a dramatic recreation of some of it in our docudrama—until Parks Canada staff at the historical park on Grosse Isle told me I had fallen for a hoax.

To me, the Keegan diary, with its oft-changed status, is the ultimate proof that whatever is the difference between fiction and non-fiction, *it is not the words or their arrangement*. Here we have a piece of fiction (novel), which became a piece of non-fiction (heretofore undiscovered authentic coffin-ship and quarantine-island diary), then turned back into a novel when the hoax was uncovered. When it purported to be fiction, it was fiction. When the same words in the same sentences purported to be non-fiction, they were non-fiction. Then the work went back to purporting to be fiction, and was fiction again.

If all of this seems to have been simpler at one time than it is now, that may be true. In the 1930s and 1940s, short fiction was a staple in many magazines, an extremely popular part of the magazine and one of the key reasons people bought, for example, *The Saturday Evening Post*. Writers could and did make solid livings writing nothing but short stories, much as TV drama and comedy writers make a good living today. To make you despair at the comparison between that state of affairs and today is not my goal; I mention it only to point out that the non-fiction writers of the 1940s and early 1950s looked across the non-fiction/fiction divide at their more popular fiction-writing cohorts, and they decided to poach some of their writing techniques. Why not import a little dialogue into a non-fiction article? Why not set a scene with description? The result was the beginning of a blurring between the two genres.

> *When Maurice Richard entered the room, in a dark suit, there was silence. People stopped conversations in mid-sentence to stare. "He hasn't changed in twenty years," said a woman beside me, and I agreed with her. He really didn't seem to have.*

The above sentences could be from a non-fictional personality profile of the late Rocket Richard, or they could be part of a scene in a short story or novel in which a fictionalized Rocket appears as a character. The fact that writers of fiction, especially those of short fiction, have delighted in giving their stories inventive new forms, such as writing them as if they were essays or letters or diaries, or salting them with made-up snippets from newspapers—well, yes, it has become more confusing.

Use the *purport* test to distinguish between fiction and non-fiction, and you should not go far wrong.

✦ ✦ ✦ Your Process

✦ Remember a favourite family anecdote—when Uncle Elmer fell in the well when he was ten and had to be rescued; when Dad snuck aboard the city bus and stayed on it all day because he was afraid to get off—whatever you have. Now write it in a paragraph or two as non-fiction. It happened. Uncle Elmer is real. Tell it like it happened.

✦ Now write the paragraphs as fiction. You're using the family anecdote as material in a short story or novel scene.

✦ Compare the difference. If there is no difference, go to a novel, any novel, and read a page, then go back and rewrite the fictional version of the anecdote until it has a more fictional feel.

...2

Novel versus Short Story

A MATTER OF LENGTH?

This is a book about fiction, and having distinguished between fiction and non-fiction in Chapter 1, I'll leave non-fiction behind and explore other distinctions, like the short story versus the novel. That is, I will try to explain the differences between the short story and the novel, as well as the creatures that exist between them and on their margins (such as the postcard story and the novella).

What's more, I am going to freely court a charge of oversimplification by saying that the distinctions are mainly based on length. Again, I have heard some lovely thoughts on the characteristics of the short story, the novella, and the novel, but most of them beg argument and can be shown to fail. I will grant that the fictional forms are different in ways other than length, but I also contend they are different because their length enforces on them different

7

demands. Clever authors satisfying those demands have given the different forms their character, but what goaded them into it was length.

Often, fiction writers at the early stages of their craft ask how long a novel is or should be. As if I knew, I say, "The novel is sixty thousand words or longer." How many pages is that? I answer two hundred pages (of about three hundred words). The upper limit for a novel? The sky.

When it comes to the short story, my answer is an average of three thousand words. I can hear fiction writers gnashing their teeth at this, including or especially some of my friends who are practitioners of the long short story. "Who says?" they cry. "What dictator decided that?" My response is that three thousand words is the average length of a short story asked for by magazines, literary quarterlies, anthologies, radio short-fiction slots, and contests. Now, I can hear the irritated fiction writers saying, "What way is that to define the size of an art form?" A lousy way, but it is also the way such things have been defined and decided forever.

Upper limit for the short story: ten thousand words.

Although some might say that this size is approaching a novella, I would point to the *New Yorker* short story, which over the years has often swelled to ten thousand words.

The short short story: a thousand to two thousand words.

The postcard story (called for mainly in postcard-story competitions): about five hundred words. The idea is to tell a story that is satisfying and complete in that brief space.

The novella should logically occupy the space between the long short story and the short novel: ten thousand words to sixty thousand words. Experience suggests it is more likely thirty thousand to forty-five thousand words.

Returning to the idea of an average story and how such things get decided, let's consider what goes in a short-fiction competition or at a literary quarterly or magazine. I once shared the short-fiction editor's role at a literary quarterly called *Dandelion* (which is still published in Calgary, Alberta). The experience consisted of driving to the office not nearly often enough and being confronted by an immense pile of brown envelopes. There was a modest honorarium paid annually for reading these submissions and choosing the ones to be published. Essentially, it was public service, volunteer work. If those envelopes had all contained ten thousand-word short stories, I would have quit. That is the simple truth of it. To get people, even people who love fiction and fiction quarterlies, to do this volunteer work, it has to be made reasonable.

It is the same with competitions. You want competent, experienced jurors, known to writers and readers—and you never will get them with a wide open word limit.

In the case of the literary quarterly, word length often has to do with how many writers can be represented in one issue. If a quarterly publishes a ten thousand-word story, that is probably all the short fiction it has room for in the issue. They could publish three stories of three thousand words instead, and that is what they usually choose to do: spread the opportunity.

In the rare case of trade magazines that publish short fiction, the word length is often influenced by advertising revenue. The fiction pages rarely have much appeal for advertisers, unless the writer is Norman Mailer or a rock star dabbling in fiction. You may not like to hear that, but if the magazine publisher is going to stay in business, the number of fiction pages must be limited.

The result? The three thousand-word short story is a fact of life. The sad part is that some of the best short-story writers work to a longer length. That is the form their artistry takes. Merna Summers of Edmonton, a past winner of the Marion Engel Award and the Katherine Anne Porter Prize for her short fiction, says she cannot satisfy herself with a story less than five thousand words. Her stories have run to ten thousand words. As a result, many opportunities are simply off limits. Such writers vie for the few spots in periodicals that will accept their story length, or their publication life will consist of books made up of long short stories.

✦ ✦ ✦ Your Process

✦ On your next visit to a good library (and apologies to those for whom this trip is not easy or frequent), visit the current periodicals section. Literary quarterlies are often found there, and they can be hard to find elsewhere. Also, a cross-section of other kinds of magazines are present, including the few that run short fiction or serialized novels. The point of this exercise is to familiarize yourself with where new fiction is found, and perhaps to entice you to subscribe to a few literary quarterlies.

✦ While at the library, check all the magazines or a representative sample, and compare the number that publish fiction to the total number. Establish a ratio (for example, three fiction publications out of twenty-four magazines).

✦ Take the quarterlies that do contain fiction and do a rough comparison of the number of pages each short story occupies. If you want a word count, you'll have to count the words on a page and multiply. You'll then have your own rule of thumb for what quarterlies are now publishing in terms of word count.

✦ Writers organizations often publish newsletters. Usually, they are willing to sell a copy to a non-member. The Internet (or the library) can be used as a source of the names of writers organizations in your area. Either by joining the organization (the cost is often a bargain and membership is usually open to anyone) or by getting sample copies of newsletters, you can find the short-fiction and novel manuscript competitions in your area. The Internet will also have other ways of tracking such things down, if you are adept at searching. The purpose here is not necessarily to get you to enter the competitions, though you may want to at some stage, but to provide another method of finding out the preferred length for published fiction. Novel manuscript competitions, you will probably find, are less restrictive about such things. They will tend to have a minimum but no maximum. Short-fiction competitions or novella competitions tend to have both.

···3

Novel versus Short Story

THERE MUST BE MORE TO IT

THAN NUMBERS

And of course there is more to it than length.

Responding to restrictions or opportunities created or dictated by length, authors have given the novel and the short story any number of shapes. The lack of an upper limit has brought about many immense novels, telling the story of a nation through the lives of many characters at a time of upheaval (for example, Tolstoy's *War and Peace*), or documenting the events of a single fictional day (like James Joyce's *Ulysses*). Then there's the *roman fleuve*, a series of novels that tells the story of generations of one family (for example, John Galsworthy's *The Forsythe Saga*). A novel can represent anything, go anywhere, and many writers have become besotted by the limitlessness of those opportunities. In Sterne's *Tristram Shandy*, which purports to be Tristram's life story, the author can't seem to get to the boy's birth. Hundreds of pages of family history and minutiae and digression go by, and the hero has yet to breathe his first breath. The book is humorous, a satire at the expense of long-winded writers who can't seem to move a story forward.

Not all novels tend to immensity, but the point is that the size and scope of the form are theoretically unlimited. The number of characters in a novel and the number of scenes cannot be limited or prescribed. Add as many as you want or need; likewise, settings or time horizons. As long as the experience you create is coherent, or in some way moving or delightful to the reader, the novel can succeed.

It has been said that the novel is a house of many rooms. As in a real house, there are limits to where you can go and still be in the house, but the choice of how to move from room to room is your own. In the novel, as house, the writer decides on the design and the number of rooms, but there is no set way for the author to move the characters and story inside that house. As long as a move makes sense to readers, then it can be made by the writer.

Because of its smaller size, the short story asks for economy from the writer, and not just an economy of words. You can't go on adding characters to a short story for long before you can no longer satisfyingly deal with them all. If you had twenty settings or six time horizons in a three thousand-word short story, you would probably not spend enough time on any of them to create a coherent experience for readers. So, you tend to limit the characters, limit the settings, restrict the time horizons, and so on.

Does this make the short story a lesser art form? Many argue the opposite: that the short story is more demanding and therefore greater. The short story is at least as great a challenge because of a stronger demand for compression. The short story is also sometimes compared to poetry because of this artful compression.

The short story is at once the oldest and the youngest of the major fictional forms. It has been described as a story that can be read at a sitting. Its obvious ancestor is the oral tale, the campfire story, that our ancestors told and retold and carried down through the generations and millennia before formal writing began. In those days before print, little pieces of valuable time existed at the end of a day or during bad weather, a time for story. The time-space was doubly limited. It had to fit the time available, and it had to fit the listener's span of attention.

As a literary form, the short story came along in the first half of the nineteenth century, well after the novel. The Americans usually claim to be its originator, with Edgar Allan Poe often credited as the father of the form. Like everything else in the history of literature, this claim is disputed. In the November 1847 *Godey's Lady's Book*, Poe wrote a writer's definition of fiction that has been quoted often since:

> A skilful artist has constructed a tale. He has not fashioned his thoughts to accommodate his incidents; but having deliberately conceived a certain single effect to be wrought, he then invents such incidents, he then combines such events, then discusses them in such a tone as may best serve him in establishing this preconceived effect. If his very first sentence not tend to the outbringing of this effect, then in his very first step he has committed a blunder. In the whole composition, there should be no word written of which the tendency, direct or indirect, is not to the one pre-established design. And by such means, with such skill and care, a picture is at length painted which leaves in the mind of him who contemplates it with a kindred art, a sense of the fullest satisfaction.

Though Poe was probably defining fiction rather than just the short story, I find his definition useful as a way to separate what novelists and short-story writers do when telling a story. The novelist can afford to invent incidents and combine effects that aren't focused on a single objective, as long as the central storyline is strong and readers never lose track of it for long. But when a short-story writer decides to digress, to create a loop off the main thrust of a story, that digression usually kills the story, or gets edited out, or survives as a weakness in the finished product. The economy of the form does, as Poe suggests, demand that everything in the story function with the core of the story.

What Poe calls "incidents," we would probably refer to as "scenes." His short-story definition in more modern words might read: *a series of scenes working together to tell a tale and/or to produce a strong effect on the reader.*

Next, I'll move on to the business of structuring those scenes to produce that effect.

✦ ✦ ✦ Your Process

- As preparation for the next two chapters, read the short stories "The Dog in the Van" by Greg Hollingshead and "Visitation" by Rachel Wyatt.

... *The Dog in the Van*

a short story by GREG HOLLINGSHEAD

It was an old blue Chevy van with newly painted white bumpers. Towards the rear of each side panel was a small plastic window in the shape of a teardrop. The van must have arrived in the parking lot each weekday morning at some time before eight-thirty because that was when the Crossleys arrived, and it was always there first. On days the Crossleys left as late as five-thirty or six it was still there; and if it were not in a different spot when they arrived the next morning they might have supposed it never moved at all.

Both windows were rolled up tight and the dog usually sat at one of them watching the Crossleys leave their car and walk the parking lot to the Arts Building. If Jan Crossley detoured to approach the van, the animal would neither bark nor look at her in the beseeching, tail-thumping way of some dogs but would pretend that anything else was more interesting: the next car arriving, a styrofoam coffee cup rolling around on the pavement, a fly dying in the dust of the dashboard.

Seeing the dog turn away from his wife, Dick Crossley thought how perfectly Kipling expresses Mowgli's humanity by his ability to stare down every animal in the jungle, but Jan cried, "Aw, he's self-conscious!"

"Come on, Jan."

"Look! He's just a baby!"

Dick took a step closer to study the animal through the muddy window. "An adolescent, actually," he said. "A mongrel. With a lot of German Shepherd in him."

"He's beautiful!"

Dick sighed and glanced up at the Arts Building. He imagined a half dozen of their colleagues watching from office windows.

"Oh Dick. I just wish we lived in the country."

Dick was looking at his watch. "Listen. I've got exactly fifteen minutes to get that Kipling lecture together."

"Dick! He's been shot!"

There was a long wound on the dog's left foreleg that looked like a graze from a .22. As they stared at the wound the dog gave its foreleg a lick and lifted pathetic eyes.

"He knew we were talking about his leg," Jan said as Dick walked her towards the Arts Building.

"Uh huh."

Usually the dog sat in the front seat of the van and was therefore visible from a distance, often before the Crossleys got out of their car. The first time Jan noticed that the dog was sitting in the driver's seat, she cried, "Look, Dick! He wants to drive away!" To which Dick replied that obviously the dog sat in whatever seat the sun shone on. When the dog was not visible he was sleeping, usually on one of the seats, paws dangling, or in the space between the seats. Occasionally, not often, he slept in the back of the van, which was more or less empty. If the dog slept in the back, Jan was able to see him only by making a visor with her hands and putting her face right up to the rear window. When she did this, Dick became anxious and walked on ahead. He was afraid that a colleague would see her or that she would startle the dog into sudden noise. He thought of dogs going wild with savage barking in the backs of parked station wagons. But nothing like that ever happened with this dog. As Jan reported to Dick, if the dog saw her he would open his eyes and close them without even lifting his head, or he would lift his head and look away as if scrutinizing the dark inner wall of the van.

One evening Jan said that Dan Cavanaugh had told her sometimes he heard howling from the van on his way to his eight o'clock class. "Dan gets here at seven in the morning," Jan said. "Which means that poor dog is locked up inside that van for eleven hours a day at the very least."

"He probably gets walked," said Dick, who was reading the paper.

"I'd be very surprised."

Dick looked up in mild amusement. "Why?"

"Because somebody who would lock a dog in a van for eleven hours a day is not likely to care if the dog goes for a walk or not."

Dick did not long consider the logic of this before he returned to the paper. "He would if the dog shat in the van."

Jan drank her coffee and gazed out at the night. "How could I find out."

"Chalk the dog's feet," Dick said, not looking up.

"Very funny."

For a long time then Dick was aware of Jan staring at the top of his head, where the hair was thinning. Finally she said, "I'll chalk the handles!"

"Oh fine. Not in broad daylight, please."

"Nobody'll notice."

The next morning Jan took a piece of chalk from one of the classrooms and went out into the parking lot and chalked the handles. That evening on their way to the car she checked and reported that they had not been touched.

"Did you do the back door?" Dick asked as they pulled out of the parking lot.

"Damn," Jan said quietly. "Tomorrow."

Complete chalking confirmed that the next day, anyway, the dog had been given no walk. That evening Jan got into the car angry. "I'm reporting this," she said. "It's not fair."

"Jan, people have been doing this kind of thing to animals for thousands of years. What's the difference between tying a dog to a stake all day and leaving it in a van?"

"That's like saying what's wrong with concentration camps when genocide happens all the time."

"It is not."

"He's got no air! He can't even walk in a proper circle! He can't go to the bathroom!"

"I'd be surprised if a dog of mine went to my bathroom!" Dick laughed, but his eyes were on Jan and they were anxious.

Jan stared out the window. "I want to complain to somebody."

"You've been complaining to me for six weeks. Is there something I'm supposed to be doing that I'm not?"

Jan looked at him, faintly startled. "What's it got to do with you?"

"Or you. I mean, aren't you getting a little obsessive about this? So somebody leaves his dog in his van. It's his dog, it's his van. The dog seems happy. The owner's probably happy. Term's almost over, so I'm happy. Why can't you be?"

"I told you. I think it's cruel."

"Call the S.P.C.A."

Jan did and was told that they would take the dog away only if it was visibly maltreated or sick.

When she complained to Dick about this response, he said, "Right. How about a petition on the windshield."

Jan considered this, her eyes studying his face, which he kept impassive. "A note," she finally said.

"Saying what."

"That I think it's inhuman."

"Inhumane?"

"Both."

"Are you sure a German Shepherd owner who drives a beat-up 1971 van with a Playboy bunny rabbit hanging from the rearview is going to even recognize what you're saying? It would probably do as much good as reading the note to the dog."

"Maybe there's a university law about pets on campus."

"Careful. The Dean's secretary brings her cat to the office. You wouldn't want to cross the Dean's secretary."

"Dick, why can't you see this?"

"I've said already, in a whole lot of different ways, why I can't see this. Jan, you're obsessed."

"Now it's my problem."

"I'm not saying the dog is not being maltreated—though I have to admit I can't see it from the animal's appearance or behaviour. I am saying that you do have this way of focussing on things and not letting them go. You're like a dog yourself, the way you're always worrying some bone—"

"Now I'm the dog."

"Jan, be reasonable."

The next day Jan called Campus Security, but they had no interest in the dog as long as it stayed in the van. They asked if the parking sticker on the windshield was valid until the end of the term. Jan went out and checked and called them back to say that it was. In that case, Campus Security said, it was no concern of theirs.

For some time Jan had been losing sleep over the dog in the van, though usually by the end of second term she had trouble sleeping anyway. She began to talk about the owner of the van, who it might be. Like Dick's, her office overlooked the parking lot. One evening she stayed on to wait for the owner to leave for the day. She kept an eye on the lot until midnight, when she fell asleep at her desk. By two a.m. the van was gone.

"It must be a student," she told Dick as she got into bed at a quarter to three, "studying for exams. Some thoughtless kid. You know that this means, don't you."

"What—" said Dick, who was not awake.

"Today that poor dog was in that van for at least seventeen hours."

Their colleagues had started making little jokes to Dick about Jan's obsession. She talked to everybody. Dick wanted the term to end so she could relax in the sun and the long evenings of summer and recover from the fatigue that had to be what caused her to narrow down like this.

"Maybe I should just confront him," Jan said one day. "Maybe he's even one of my students. Maybe I should offer to take his dog for a walk. You know what some of their schedules are like. And this term I've got that two hour break—"

"Don't confront the owner," Dick said wearily. "Don't offer to walk his dog for him. Support the S.P.C.A., leave a note of outrage on the windshield, get up a petition, buy a handgun and shoot the dog, but do not confront the owner."

"Why are you being so impatient with me?"

"Because it's all I ever hear from you— Jan? Here's an idea. We'll get another dog. A small one like Fergie. How would that be?"

Two years previous they had bought a Lakeland terrier, but one Sunday morning it was hit by a car. Dick could still see Jan bawling up the driveway in her nightgown holding the smashed little thing in her outstretched hands. It was like something out of Greek tragedy.

"No," she now said carefully. "I think we should live in the country before we get another dog."

"Right. It's a sign. We'll move to the country. We've talked about this for three years. We'll move to the country and buy a proper dog. A big dog. We'll teach evenings, three days a week, avoid rush hours—"

"Dick? Moving to the country is not the point here."

"What is the point."

"I'm worried about the dog."

One warm morning in April, in the last week of lectures, they arrived to find one of the van's windows open and the dog asleep in the sun on the pavement by the front wheel. They parked nearby, and the sound of their slamming doors had the dog on its feet, ready to bolt. They approached cautiously, because its face as it stood sniffing the air told nothing of what it would do. But it was still sniffing the back of Jan's hand as she placed the other on its neck then scratched and rubbed behind its ears. When Jan stood up she held her fingers under Dick's nose. They smelled of dog. Dick drew back. The dog was stretching, its back legs straight out behind, its mouth in a grimace, and in that position, at the very height of its stretch, it fell over.

"He's sick!" Jan cried, kneeling beside the dog.

"Don't touch it! Get back!"

The dog's eyes opened. It looked at Jan and Dick a moment then straight ahead, as if concentrating. Its paws twitched once, twice. One eye seemed to swell. It made no attempt to move.

Dick had pulled Jan to her feet, and now they stood, his hands at her shoulders, staring down at the dog. Their briefcases lay on the pavement behind them. A cool breeze came across the pavement. It flattened a section of the animal's fur.

Suddenly the dog scrambled to its feet, panting. With its tail going, its muzzle crinkled, its lips lifted off its yellow teeth, it came slowly, possibly unsteadily, towards Jan. Dick pulled her back, muttering, "Let's get out of here."

Jan let herself be walked away. The dog stood watching them go. Twice it barked, tail going, as if it thought they were playing, and then it circled to lie down again in the sun.

"He was smiling," Jan said as Dick hurried her into the building. "Have you ever seen a dog smile before?"

"Dog's don't smile."

"Maybe falling over is a trick he can do—"

"Like drawing blood," Dick said. "I'm calling the S.P.C.A. You don't take chances with rabies. It lives in the country. Sometimes there's mud on the tires. It's probably been bitten by a fox, or a skunk."

Dick phoned the S.P.C.A., and when the Crossleys left that afternoon at 3:30, the dog was gone. Jan insisted they leave a note on the windshield explaining what had happened.

"OK. Just don't sign it or give our number."

That was Thursday. The weekend was Easter. On Saturday Jan called the S.P.C.A., but they had no record of the dog. She was told that if she wanted to claim it she would have to come and identify it. "What if they've already put him down and he wasn't sick?" she asked Dick.

Dick took her hand. "Jan, it's Easter Sunday, and tomorrow's Easter Monday. Why don't we relax. We won't think about the dog. Wherever it is at this moment, it almost certainly is not in the van. And they don't put down healthy dogs who haven't bitten anybody." At least, Dick did not think so.

On Tuesday they did not have to be at the university until ten-thirty. When they arrived the dog was back in the van.

"I am so relieved!" Jan cried. This time when she approached, the dog barked happily. In shock Dick saw her hand go to the door handle and the door open. The dog jumped down past her and came wagging over to him, sniffing at his crotch. Dick stepped back.

"Come on, boy," Dick said. "Back in the van—"

"Oh, Dick. Please. Let's let him walk around a bit."

Dick left Jan in the parking lot rubbing the dog's neck. He imagined rushing her to the hospital for stitches and shots.

When they left at three, the dog was asleep on the pavement by the driver's side. "There. See?" Dick said. "The owner's been by."

"I left a note," Jan explained quickly as she went over to give the dog a scratch. "I said we wouldn't call anybody if he could just not be locked up in the van all the time."

Dick rolled his eyes and walked on.

On a dim afternoon later that week Dick was on his way to the library to return books. He was in a hurry because it was going to rain. As he passed the Java Joint he noticed Jan sitting with a young guy in a denim jacket. She saw Dick through the window and waved.

"Dick, this is Larry. It's his dog."

Larry had worked hard to develop his upper body, which he carried like something blown in glass. His fine blond hair had been done by a hairdresser. He wore a gold necklace, a ring with an amethyst in it, and a massive I.D. bracelet. He had pale blue eyes, a squarish, handsome face, and a little tick of a sunburned nose.

"Hello, Larry," Dick said as they shook hands. "Jan's been worried about that dog of yours."

"She told me," Larry said. "I just hate like heck to leave Mr. D alone all day, but you guys should see my timetable, eh?"

"Larry's in Business," Jan said. Her eyes were anxious.

Dick did not like the look of Larry. "When it fell over," he told him, "we thought it had rabies, I hope you didn't mind—"

"Oh, no problem. I just swung down on Saturday and picked him up. He was one freaked-out pup."

"What was it?"

"What."

"Why did your dog fall over?"

Larry shrugged. "Like I was telling your wife. Hey, there's nothing Mr. D likes better than a super-good scratch."

"D for dog," Jan explained.

"No, Larry," Dick said. "It fell over."

Larry shook his head. He sure did not know anything about that.

"Maybe its leg gave out," Dick suggested irritably. "It was shot, wasn't it?"

"Aw yeah," Larry replied. "That was just a graze, eh. He's sure a-scared of loud noises now though."

"What did the S.P.C.A. say?"

"Oh, they said he's fine. Really good."

When Dick noticed that he was standing talking to this mendacious fool with an armful of heavy books, he excused himself and ducked out, hunching to protect the books as if the rain had already started. It was so like Jan to try to handle everything on her crackbrained idea of a human level. Never mind the time and emotion she wasted, or that it was none of her business, or that Larry was nobody to have coffee with.

Dick barely had time to get back to the Arts Building before the storm hit. High in his office he stood and watched the rain come down and the lightning glare white and flicker for long seconds. There were great cracks of thunder like rock splitting, rumbling declensions of sound that shook the air. Suddenly a flash of brown at the passenger window of the van caught Dick's eye, and when he looked he saw the dog's face smash against the window and disappear, smash against the window and disappear.

After hesitating, Dick carefully unfolded the plastic raincoat he kept in his desk drawer and went down to the van. At close range the violence of the dog's terror was frightening. The animal was whimpering like a caught pup, it was frothing and bleeding at the mouth and nose. When it saw Dick its eyes fixed his for just a moment before it smashed its head and body against the window.

Immediately then it disappeared into the rear of the van. Dick placed a hand on the passenger door. The dog hit the back doors. Dick pressed the handle. The passenger door opened. Quickly he slammed it. A second later the dog hit it at full force. Dick stepped back shaking. He was getting soaked. In fifteen or twenty minutes the storm would be over. He turned and walked back to the Arts Building. Larry would have to look after his own dog.

Safe in his office Dick watched the storm pass. The dog was out of sight now, probably in the back of the van licking its wounds. The clouds were sliding away, the sky was deep blue beyond, and the cars in the parking lot were glistening with a million points of light. Dick's eyes fell on a happy-looking couple crossing the lot. It was Jan and Larry, coming back from coffee. Larry was being exuberant, with large gestures. Jan was looking at him. Her head was held on one side, and she was smiling and laughing at whatever it was he was saying. When they reached the van, Larry did an exaggerated finger-to-the-lips pantomime and they both took a quick peek through the rear window. He then led her away towards the front of the van, where he put into operation a succession of elaborate delay tactics. It was nearly ten minutes that she lingered there, the two of them engaged in a complicated, lover-like, public dance of prolonged leave-taking. And then, when they finally parted— Jan really was walking back to the Arts Building, Larry really had got into his van— and Dick was about to turn away from the window, Larry's square, anguished face popped above the van's roof and he called to her. But Jan must have already entered the building and not heard, because Larry stared after her only a few seconds before ducking back into the van and roaring out of the parking lot.

Dick made sure that the door of his office was open an inch. He then sat at his desk and moved paper around with trembling hands until he heard Jan come down the hall from the mail room and go into her office. On the ride home and at dinner she seemed distracted, as usual, but unnaturally happy. She had nothing to say about Larry. When Dick asked casually what he was like she looked quizzical and said, "You met him. You saw what he was like." Dick did not tell her that Larry had called to her. He did not want her to know he had been watching.

The van was not in the lot the next day, or the next. Jan became worried. "That's funny," she said as they got into the car on the second day. "Larry told me he had to study all this week."

"Your Larry's a liar," Dick said.

The next day, by purest chance, Dick was outside Jan's office when her phone rang. He stopped to listen. It was Larry. Dick stepped into Jan's office and closed the door. "No," he said. "You will not talk to Larry." He took the receiver from Jan's hand and replaced it.

"Dick, what are you doing?"

"This whole thing has gone far enough."

"What whole thing?"

"I saw you, the whole rigmarole. You're my wife, Jan."

"What are you talking about?"

When the phone rang again Dick put his hand on the receiver so that Jan could not pick it up. When it rang a third time he lifted the receiver and said, "Larry, you little creep. Harass my wife again and I'll have you out of this university on your ass." The phone did not ring again.

There followed two and a half days of tension and talk, tension and talk. At the end of the third day Jan apologized for being "too friendly" with Larry, while Dick acknowledged that he had "possibly overreacted."

The following morning the van was back, but the dog was not visible in the front seat. Jan went directly to the rear window and made a visor with her hands. "He's here!" she called happily, and opened the doors.

The dog jumped down past her and trotted straight around the side of the van towards Dick. Its front legs were bandaged, it held its head to one side as if curious, and as it rose towards him, Dick could see its muzzle lifted off its yellow teeth in what looked like a crinkled smile.

• • •

... *Visitation*

a short story by RACHEL WYATT

Almeida went to answer the door hoping it was a stranger come to tell her that it had all been a mistake. *That was not your daughter, Mrs. Kerwell. Your child is alive and well and will be home tomorrow.* Or maybe on the other side of the door stood a relative of the man Harriet had been with, the man who died with his arms round her. The man whose name they didn't yet know. His sister perhaps, who would speak hesitantly and later embrace her and tell her all about him.

But the woman who stood on the step was familiar and walked into the house without being asked and spoke right out.

"Hello, Almeida. Don't you recognise me? It's me. Martha. Sapph. I'd no end of trouble to find you. Couldn't remember your married name. It was Gerry in the end. Remembered her married name. That wedding."

"Come in. Well. My goodness, Martha. Come in. Sit down."

"Twelve years. I've changed."

"Dad's funeral."

"That's right. When they buried your Dad that day, I had a feeling a whole lot of deer and moose gave a sigh of relief. But. Sorry. I mean, you know. It was a sad time. And this is a sad time."

Almeida had got out of bed that morning, put on her clothes like a wind-up doll, made orange juice, remembered her mother saying that it was as easy to make a table look nice as not and got out the lace cloth and the plates with the leaf design and had sat across the table from Joe, tried to eat, tried to admire the sunny morning. And felt nothing. Now she felt surprise. And a need to be hospitable. She looked at her cousin's face, held the resemblance for a moment.

"I'll get you some coffee."

"I'd like that."

"You're looking well."

"I've come to say I'm sorry. About Harriet."

"I'll get the coffee. You just sit here."

Almeida leaned against the counter in the kitchen. The backyard looked as though an army of gophers had moved in. The beds all upturned, flowers, bulbs, scattered. For days, Joe had spent time out there digging the beds over. And over. For all the world like a gravedigger. That thought came into her head before she could stop it and the tears followed. At least he wasn't out there now. She pushed the button on the kettle and then recalled it had no water in it. All right to burn the house down but not to kill this apparently kind visitor.

Yesterday, to pass the time, she'd made a plum coffee cake and they'd both eaten a scrap of it. She'd been planning to give it to people who still had an appetite for food or put it in the freezer. Along with their feelings, hers and Joe's. Likewise frozen. Their lives were a tableau with no future beyond the day they'd returned from China laden with silk and memories. June twenty-fourth, the day of darkness.

"I'd've come to the funeral but I didn't hear till last Wednesday," Martha shouted from the other room.

"What do you take in your coffee?" Almeida called back and then, remembering her mother again, got out the cut glass milk jug and matching sugar bowl. But Martha had come into the kitchen now and was standing behind her. A scent of lemon and carnations came with her.

"I should've said, Almy. It was the shock of seeing you. I don't drink coffee. Tea. Herb tea if you've got it. And yum, some of that delicious looking cake."

In the back of the shelf was a little bag of something called *Sensualitea*. Almeida poured hot water over a couple of spoonfuls and hoped it wouldn't have any effect on Martha, at least till she got home. She had in the old days been a sexy woman.

Though this fiftyish person with her rosy cheeks, clear eyes, rounded body, had little to do with the Sapphire who'd danced in gauzy veils at the Blue Donkey. *Fine*, was the word for this woman. *Healthy* was another. *Gaudy* another still. Dark red jacket, dark red skirt, gold blouse in soft summer material, chunky gold jewellery. She brought colour to the drab house. Almeida silently thanked her for not wearing black.

They sat down with their drinks and Almeida passed her visitor a slice of coffee cake on a plate, and a fork.

"How's Joe taking it?"

What did she expect? If Martha had come to ask the usual appalling questions, Almeida would pull her up, snatch the cake away and push her down the steps.

"You were selling real estate, Martha, last I heard."

"Briefly. The business world is not for me."

"What are you doing now?"

"Erwin and I."

"Erwin?"

"Erwin sent me really. Though I would've come anyway. Erwin and I invested together in a few acres north of Aurora. We guide people to healthy attitudes. Not happiness, Almeida. Nothing unrealistic like that. Erwin always says that if God had meant us to be happy, he'd've given us four legs and a tail and the ability to leave large pats of shit in fields for people to step in."

Almeida wondered why, in her deep distress, this vision had been sent to her. She looked at Martha and yes, she was real, she was there, she was eating a mouthful of coffee cake and the crumbs were spilling onto her lap and from there to the floor.

"How do you make this?"

"The usual way. As long as the plums are firm there's no problem with it."

"Mmm. You could give me the recipe."

Almeida waited. Dark times allowed for this. Every now and then a clown appeared on the stage to distract, annoy, leave you feeling worse off. This time a clown with a painted face and a big red smile.

"So what we do, me and Erwin, we take in the disturbed, people in sorrow, and we offer them alternatives, another way of seeing what they see."

Almeida helped herself to a good-sized piece of cake. No way she could get through this conversation without nourishment.

"We'd make room for you and Joe. A week at our place, only six hundred dollars. A reduction for relatives. I could tell you stories of our successes."

The bite of cake stuck in Almeida's esophagus. It would never go down, she knew it. Like a stone it lay there and would be there when they buried her.

Martha's eye lighted on the photograph of Harriet in her hiking outfit.

"She was brave, eh. To go and do what she did. And all that among strangers."

To stop her, Almeida nearly shouted, "We were sorry to hear about your Dad."

"Dad. Oh yes. Well it's ages ago. He'd've been ninety-seven next month. He used to ask after you Almeida. Always a soft spot."

Wrong diversion. Almeida didn't want right now to think about Uncle George. But Martha continued.

"When your Dad married your Mom, it hurt him so much. He told me all about it."

"Told you?"

"I am his daughter, Almy. And you were kind of like her, like your mother. It drove him crazy. Love is the weirdest thing. By the time he married my Mom, he'd mainly gotten over it. Marge never forgave him, did she? I guess that was obvious. All those years of her life. The whole thing had a kind of warping effect on him. That and the war."

There were tortures of various degrees. Being led through her own past by a relation who saw it all differently and some parts of it up close was a cruelty on this day. Why not the rack, oh Lord! Why not a plague of frogs!

"How's Sue?"

"Sue has her life. I have mine."

Thoughts of her sister stopped Martha in her flow but not for long.

"She's taken on this martyr role. The only one who does anything for Mom! I just do what I do more quietly that's all. Did you and Jess have this problem? Well I guess your parents passed on—I mean before it came to arguing about who looked after them."

At least, and Almeida couldn't stop the thought coming into her mind, my daughters now won't be arguing about that. To hold back her tears she found another question.

"Tell me more about your—what is it? Retreat?"

"First and foremost is nourishment. That's my department. Nothing like sitting down to a nice meal, well set out, to take people out of their trouble. We run our sessions from Monday to Friday and the Monday dinner is always the same. Blue cheese soufflé, appetizer. Fish, the best we can get that day, main course. Salmon, sole, cod Provencal. And then Pear Hélène. You can't serve mousse if you've started with soufflé. Or it might be chocolate praline pie. It's not really a pie. Pear Hélène is the favourite. And on Mondays, the wine is free."

Almeida wanted to cry out, what has this to do with my daughter? My loved child? But she sat and let the images of food dangle there between them.

"We're careful about coffee. Stimulants can add to grief. And basically we're out to soothe."

"After nourishment?"

"On Tuesdays we serve red meat. We like people to approach their anger."

Almeida saw herself stalking her anger as a beast through the jungle, hissing and growling, setting traps for it, having it turn on her when, finally, she came face to face with it.

"We offer a course on grief control."

A dam. A dyke. Great turbines turning grief into electricity, fuelling a city, a use for it at last. And out there some Doctor Strangelove inducing grief in people because the industrial world needed cheap energy. She and Joe grieving for the sake of streetlights, or perhaps, for a rock band. Keeping the guitars and the synthesizer going at full blast.

"Do you get a lot of clients? Customers?"

"We're full till September."

"People know in advance that they're going to be in mourning? In trouble?"

"We make space for immediate problems. We are elastic. What I could do for you and Joe."

"I don't think we're quite ready."

"Almeida. I don't want you to think I just came to drum up business."

"No Martha, no."

And for a moment, Almeida saw a look of Uncle George, a kindness and sympathy, in the face opposite, but it disappeared quickly, and there was the crafty look of the old Sapphire who knew her audience and responded to it by taking off another veil.

"Is Joe in?"

"He had—has some business to attend to." He was with Geraldine at the bank sorting out Harriet's affairs. She'd offered to go too but he'd shaken his head and gone out without a word.

"Did Jess come to the funeral?"

Now she wanted a list of the mourners!

"Jess has a bad back. She fell, slipped on something in her apartment."

"I see."

"She and Harriet were close. She would have come if she could. She's in a lot of pain."

"I guess I shouldn't be too long. But now we're in touch. Erwin says family is very important. Nothing takes its place."

"How did you meet Erwin?" Almeida asked, having in mind a long-haired evangelical swindler.

"I was standing on the street corner not knowing which way to turn and there he was. It was the eyes you know. He has these piercing eyes that look deep into you. I haven't reached the depth of him yet. I may never but I'm enjoying the looking. He's a lot younger than I am but we don't find that a problem. People take me for his mother. He's very good about the place. The heavy work."

She was still Sapphire. The tales of Uncle George's life with his second wife and their two daughters might well have been true. But maybe it was Uncle George's own nature that created his difficulties. The women in his life had not had an easy time of it either.

Martha leaned forward and said, "Family is family, Almy, and whatever we've done or not done in the past I want you to know that my sympathy is with you. The loss of a child."

Almeida's only desire was to end the visit before the scream she was holding back rose to the surface. She stood up and moved towards the door.

"It was good of you to come," she said.

"Now I've found you."

"We'll be going away soon."

"I'll leave these brochures with you. Think about it. It might be just what you need."

"Goodbye, Martha. Give my regards to Erwin."

Anger. That was what Almeida knew she was feeling as she closed the door. All these people figuring what they needed right now, she and Joe. Casseroles, company, cards, flowers, calls. And that woman had come here in her bright clothes, had deliberately sought them out in their distress. Made an effort. Looked for them. So that she too could oppress, take away with her a little of their own sorrow and share it. With somebody called Erwin for Chrissake! And all she and Joe wanted was time with Harriet, the one thing they couldn't have.

She sat down and all the tears she'd been holding back since the day of the funeral poured out of her. She grabbed a cloth and held it to her face. She felt herself shaking and didn't try to stop. Empty, exhausted, the cloth soaked, her hands damp, she heard the door open. She ran upstairs and washed her face, changed her sweater and went down to face the rest of the day.

She said to Joe, "You just missed my cousin Martha."

"They all come, don't they," he replied.

"I'll go get something for dinner," she said. "And we'll go for a walk tomorrow. Next week, we'll have Gerry and the family round."

He looked up and gave her his best attempt at a smile.

"I'll fix the swing."

She began to say that Sharon and Tyler were grown and their legs would touch the ground but instead she said, "They'll like that."

Joe said, "It will get light again. One of these days."

She knew he was right.

She reached for her recipe book and found the page she wanted. Danish blue, butter, milk, eggs. More fat than she and Joe were supposed to eat. But with a salad. Brown bread. The soufflé dish with the green fluted edge. She set the book down sharply. For several minutes sorrow had released its grip on her. How could she do that? Withdraw all that grief from Harriet? A calmer voice said, *Harriet doesn't know. Harriet is not aware.*

"I won't be long, Joe," she said.

She stepped outside into the heat. The air smelt of sulphur. There was traffic, there were people, there were young women. She wanted to go back into the house and close the door and hide from anyone who might come up to her and say the terrible words she'd heard so often lately. *Life must go on.* But she went out and walked along the street to the store because nothing was more important right then than to buy four ounces of blue cheese.

• • •

··· 4
Traditional Story Structure

Nothing excites more outright anger in a fiction writer than being told there is a form into which the short story does or should fit. The word *formula* comes to mind, and it is insulting to an artist that his or her work should ever be dictated by formula.

The story structure fed to us in high school, and in a lot of books about writing, especially on writing for film and television, goes like this. When the story begins, your character is doing what she or he always does: going to school or work, or tending the babies, or getting ready for another launch of the space shuttle. Then something happens that fractures the routine. A beautiful man or woman arrives to sell a vacuum cleaner. A husband arrives home with a dog. A teenage daughter brings home her boyfriend, saying that he will live in her room from now on.

The ordinary way of things at the start is called by some *the opening equilibrium*. The thing that happens to break it is the *point of attack*. The story then goes in search of a solution to the problem, or some would say it searches for a new equilibrium. The main character tries to solve the problem created at the point of attack and moves through a couple of minor crises en route to the major climax, the highest point of action in the story, where the game is won or lost, solved or left unresolved forever. The story ends once we know the results of the climax. Sometimes it is said that the main character must be changed by the events of the story.

We all know this old dramatic arc, and most of us hate it, enemy of ingenuity and creativity that it is. A shape like a roof, an inverted V, lopsided to the right. Let's burn it in a bonfire on the summer solstice, while people dance around holding hands.

In the world of television, especially in books about how to write for television and become fabulously well-to-do, there is no shilly-shallying about the dramatic arc. It not only has to be there in a TV or film script, but the right parts of it have to arrive at certain minutes in the hour or half-hour television slot— so we can go to commercial. The description of the arc appears in books about how to write TV drama, usually differentiated according to the metaphor chosen to describe it. Sometimes, your hero is said to be in a boat on a river. The river curves, hits several sets of rapids, each with more dangerous rocks and white-water than the last. Oops, here comes a submerged tree! And, finally, hang onto your hat: the waterfall! The character drowns or is saved, and that's your story.

Another memorable metaphor from film and TV is that you put your hero in a tree, throw rocks at him or her for an hour, then let the poor soul out of the tree. Whatever the arc is likened to—a river, a walk across the Gobi Desert, a voyage to the moon—the shape is the same, the idea is the same, the dogma is the same. Interestingly, writers tend to be more forgiving of the notion of a formula story when thinking about writing for television, perhaps because they have heard that writing drama for television is lucrative, as opposed to the artistic purity and poverty in most every other part of the writing game.

I am all for ignoring the dramatic arc, provided we know and acknowledge one thing: that the dramatic arc is the natural shape of a great many stories, in fact most of the stories that have ever been told on this planet. When the oral storytellers from whom we all descend thought about how they might tell a story, they realized that they needed to begin by getting the listeners' attention. Then they needed to hold onto it. That required the story to become more exciting along the way. At the end, they needed to pay off the story with some happening bigger or more emotionally powerful than the rest. Finally came the need for it all to be important somehow.

Ever since, writers of fiction and drama have tended to stick with that way of telling a story—because of how effectively it lures, excites, and satisfies an audience.

Am I advocating that you write your stories that way? No. I don't strive to follow the pattern myself. Why should you? But I am advocating that you understand why that form of story has been so tiresomely enduring. However you orchestrate your fictional text, you will confront the need for something that makes the story move and urges the reader to move with it. A question will exist, and readers will want the answer badly enough to read on. A mood will be created that is so evocative readers will want to stay in it for the sheer sensual pleasure or melancholy. A fictional character, made to live in readers' imaginations, will try to do something interesting or compelling or creepy, and readers will go along to see what happens.

John Gardner, in his wonderful book *The Art of Fiction*, used the term *propulsion:* that which intrigues, compels, seduces the reader into moving forward. The force of propulsion in a story can be of any strength except ineffectively weak. The strength of it may be the strength of your reader's engagement with your story. It may determine the power of the experience.

◆ In your first reading of "The Dog in the Van" and "Visitation," I hope you were reading for story rather than studying form. Now, read the stories a second time to see if they conform to the traditional story structure or if they have a different form. Do they conform in some ways and not in others?

◆ While rereading the stories, stop every few paragraphs and ask yourself what is propelling you forward as a reader. What is it that you are trying to find out? What enticements beyond simple plot are acting on you?

Under the Golden Arc

GOING DEEPER

Your process for the last chapters called for you to read, and then reread, the short stories "The Dog in the Van" and "Visitation," and to make an assessment of whether they fit the dramatic arc, the traditional shape of a story.

In Greg Hollingshead's "The Dog in the Van," from his collection *White Buick*, the Crossleys, husband and wife, work at a university. One day, Jan notices a dog locked in a white van in their parking lot. The van is there before them. It leaves after they leave. When they first notice it, the dog has a graze mark—a bullet wound, maybe—on its leg. This moment could be of no consequence in the lives of many, but Jan Crossley is deeply affected by this dog, deeply concerned.

For Jan, checking on the dog becomes part of what she does. Her interest, her worry, grows until it verges on obsession. Or that's how Dick Crossley sees it. He would rather ignore the dog as someone else's business.

At the story's centre, there is a problem: the welfare of an abused dog. In the traditional story arc, a problem, identified near the beginning, intensifies. If we ask does the problem of the dog get more difficult and complicated in this story, the answer is, yes, it certainly does.

Jan ascertains that the dog is locked in the van for as many as seventeen hours a day. Then a day arrives when the dog is out on the pavement tied to the wheel, an improvement, but when Jan approaches the dog, it has a fit and falls over. She calls the SPCA. The dog disappears. The next time the dog shows up in the van, Jan is more relieved than angry.

Then Jan meets the owner of the dog, Larry, and amazingly, they get on well—too well as far as Dick is concerned. Finally, in a violent electrical storm, Dick sees that the dog is throwing itself against the windows of the van in fear. In the story's biggest scene, Dick attempts to help the dog. He gets as far as the van in the storm, sees the dog leaving bloody smears on the glass from smashing its body there. He opens the door, but slams it quickly closed, just as the dog's body crashes against it. Dick walks away, repeating the belief with which he began this story: the dog is not his problem. Now, he absolutely means it.

After this climax, Jan seems inclined to continue the friendship with Larry, but Dick won't stand for it. He won't allow her to even speak to Larry on the phone, and that is seemingly the end of it, except that the dog is in the van in the parking lot at the end of the story, still part of their lives.

Without straining too hard, you can see the traditional structure in the story of the dog and the van. The story has an early development that shatters the main character's equilibrium and creates the problem. The search for a solution moves from crisis to crisis. The action is always rising. Finally, it comes to a climax. But however easy this rising and climaxing structure is to decipher and map, it is also a deception. Unlike a *Lassie* episode, this story is not about a dog. It is the story of a marriage going wrong.

In creative writing classes the world over, a frequent question is: Whose story is it? At first glance, promoted by the deception of the traditional arc that stands above it as its primary feature, "The Dog in the Van" might seem to be the dog's story. But if that were the case, the story would end with some transforming incident in the life of the dog. The dog would die. The dog would decide to move in with the Crossleys. The dog would run away. But what ends the story is the confrontation between the married couple, because the story has been about them all along (and more about Dick than about Jan).

What the dog is to the story is its *catalyst*. From the moment the dog enters their lives, it forces upheaval. It reveals opposing values. It forces them into collision. Jan's natural instinct is to throw herself into the problem, ready to inconvenience, even endanger, herself to help the dog. She knows what is right for the dog, and she wants to see justice done. Dick's attitude is that, though he doesn't wish the dog ill, he doesn't want any involvement with it. Everything Jan says about helping the dog, or understanding the problem, Dick counters with a statement about how its circumstances may not be as serious as they seem; how inevitably it is the owner's dog, not theirs, and that they should stay out of it— meaning Jan should stay out of it. It is not far-fetched to say that this story is about Dick's need to control Jan and about her need not to be controlled.

By the end of the story, the dog is even more than a catalyst. It has become the language of Dick and Jan's marriage, the language Dick is attempting to speak when he tries and fails to help the dog in the storm. He is speaking it again when he demands that Jan not go on any further with Larry as a friend. Finally, the story speaks back to Dick in the language of the dog. At the end, the dog, still part of his life after his many attempts to be rid of it, comes to him and smiles.

To some extent short stories can be sorted into those that rely on rising action, suspense, and climax for their structure and those where the movement in the story is toward a new understanding. Both kinds of movement can be present in a story, woven together, and this is the case with "The Dog in the Van."

Let's look at the story again as a progression toward new understanding. Jan's desire to help the dog is simply that: a desire to help the dog. She even has to say as much to Dick when he implies that she is acting out some kind of pantomime whose meaning is that she wants a replacement for their own dog: a dog that was killed.

"I want to help the dog," she says.

If Jan's goal is to help the dog in the van, can Dick say that his desire is as simple as not wanting to help the dog? His motivation is more convoluted and harder to pin down. He wants to avoid complication in his life and commitment to anything that might turn messy. He is full of fear of the dog and of its unseen owner. When the dog keels over, Dick thinks rabies. When Jan wants to confront the owner, Dick imagines some criminal, capable of harming them.

But above all, Dick is full of criticism of the way Jan does things. She's like a dog herself, he even suggests at one point, in her singularity of focus. She imagines the dog has emotions the dog doesn't have. She is easily obsessed.

When he goes to the van in the storm, what is Dick trying to do? Is he trying to confront his fear and surmount it? Is he trying to gain Jan's approval so she will prefer him over Larry? Or is he just trying to help the dog? He is certainly not following his rule of staying out of things.

And, finally, he is changed by it: not by his success at helping the dog, but by his failure to do so. Instead of trying to convince Jan to stop with the dog and its owner by circuitous and often deceitful argument, Dick comes right out and demands it. To his satisfaction at least, he is facing up to the way things really are between Jan and him, and he is facing up to the way he is. He is not a reasonable, calm man who can accept the tribulations life throws at him or the eccentricities of his wife. He is brittle and bothered, and not very brave, and he might as well let it all hang out.

But having done so, the world will not necessarily go along with what Dick wants. Jan is not necessarily convinced or changed by his wish to change her. And the dog has not gone anywhere.

In the beginning decades of its life as a literary form, the short story adhered to the traditional dramatic arc and the bang-up ending we call a climax. Around the turn of the twentieth century, things changed. In James Joyce's only book of short stories, *Dubliners*, he replaced the traditional action climax with what he called "the epiphany," a moment in the life of a fictional character after which all is different, even if the moment itself is barely noticeable to others. In a story called "The Little Cloud," the epiphany is the protagonist's sudden failure of patience with his baby. He's been left to sit with the baby by his wife. The baby will not stop crying. He gives it a big shake. Everyone including the reader and "the little cloud" himself would say such an act is completely out of character for him. Now, on the other side of this epiphany, it is not. It has undeniably happened. In one of my short stories, I call these points of epiphany "the small hinges where life bends sharply."

In the Hollingshead story, the action/adventure/suspense arc (involving the dog) and the subtle move into greater self-awareness, the Joycean epiphany (involving Dick's understanding of himself and his ways within his marriage) work in tandem. If you study modern short fiction, looking for these features, you will find many stories with this plurality of structure, and you'll notice as well many catalysts. I can remember two stories where the catalyst was a household infestation of bugs. As it gets out of control, the problem of the bugs weighs on the family, reveals the flaws in the marriage. In one of my stories, "Bill's Sperm Count," a sperm test that Bill can never seem to get around to becomes the catalyst that reveals the flaws in and ends a marriage.

Before we leave "The Dog in the Van" and move on to "Visitation," another relationship between "The Dog in the Van" and the traditional structure of stories is worth pointing out. Because the traditional structure of drama is so drilled into our heads (about four times nightly for those who watch a lot of TV), a fiction writer can bargain against readers' expectations. There is a lot of playfulness in the way "The Dog in the Van" does this, much dramatic irony in the progression of events. The traditional expectation for the dog in the van is that things will go from bad to worse. Against this expectation, the dog is suddenly out of the van one day and tied to the wheel. (It's not much of an improvement, admittedly, but the dog, the Crossleys, and the readers will take what they can get.) Then just when things are looking up, they look down. The dog falls over. Sick.

Later, the story bargains against several expectations concerning the owner of the dog. First, we assume the owner will be a fiend, a pet-abusive violent criminal. We also assume that Jan will hate him, and, because Dick disagrees with Jan's every thought and decision, that Dick will at least pretend to like him. What happens is that Dick stumbles on Jan and Larry having a merry chat. Larry is reasonable. Jan likes him. They share an interest in the well-being of the dog (as compared to Dick, who is always insisting he does not care). The story's problem shifts suddenly from Jan's interest in the dog to Jan's interest in Larry. The humour of these shifts would not be possible if it weren't for readers' assumptions that stories will unfold according to the ancient rules of storytelling.

Rachel Wyatt's "Visitation" is part of a linked short-story collection Mona Lisa Smiled a Little, in which the main character, Almeida, decides to leave her husband of many years, Joe, and live alone. She discovers just how conservative her family and the world are about an older woman's quest for freedom and a better life.

The story "Visitation" is about the grief Almeida and Joe experience when one of their two daughters dies. The story is a good example of how much can happen in a story without resort to any kind of action/adventure/suspense arc at all. It shows that, without leaving the house, a story can still emotionally intensify into something almost unbearable, can still lead you on with questions about what will come next. In a story of action and suspense, the questions are typically about how to escape or what the bad guy will do next. The questions in a literary short story like "Visitation" tend to be closer to those asked in everyday life. Almeida (and readers) wonders what Almeida's cousin Martha wants with her. Is it possible that she really is there to sell her grieving cousin a stay on a health farm? What will Almeida do to get rid of her?

One of the great sources of power in good literary fiction is that readers create fictional lives and fictional dilemmas of such fidelity to the world that we can imagine ourselves in them, and that is what produces the spell of fiction, the *suspension of disbelief* that allows us to enter the fiction and feel pain and elation along with the characters.

It would also be wrong to say that "Visitation" has no relationship to the traditional structure of drama because it happens over a piece of cake instead of on K-2. Rachel Wyatt demonstrates the opposite: that a story can create dramatic tension out of escalating agony brought on by the clueless conversational gaffes of another. The story is about grieving, and all the silly things that others do to allegedly relieve us of pain that can't be relieved; pain from which we don't even want relief. What we want is for Superman to fly backward around the world reversing its spin, as he did to reverse time and bring Lois Lane back from the dead. Failing that, we don't want a casserole in a covered dish. We don't want visitors with an agenda.

For the sake of drama, Cousin Martha turns her visit into a device of torture that she twists tight and then tighter. "Martha had come to ask the usual appalling questions," thinks Almeida. Then later, "Every once in a while a clown appeared on the stage, to distract, annoy, leave you feeling worse off." And still later, "Why not the rack, oh Lord! Why not a plague of frogs!" There is an escalation happening: an escalation of pain inside Almeida. It searches for an ending, a way to stop the pain.

And that's before Martha begins to sell the merits of her and Erwin's rest farm for the grieving.

Readers looking for a climax of the exterior dimensions of an electrical storm and a self-damaging dog won't find it. As Almeida said, the clown came; the clown annoyed, distracted, and left her feeling worse—except that, in the Joycean sense, an epiphany is signalled by Almeida's being subtly different after Martha goes. All her anger over the sympathetic acts she has been putting up with roars to the surface. She sits down and cries until exhausted. Then Joe comes home. She focuses his attention on a practical task, fixing the swing for their grandchildren. She then puts all her thoughts and energies into making a blue-cheese soufflé that her cousin said was on the menu of the grief farm. Somehow, inadvertently and ironically, the cousin has in some small way helped Almeida move to the next stage of pain.

Returning to the way that our in-built dramatic arc machine supplies assumptions about how the story will unfold, and how a good writer will bargain against those assumptions to achieve surprise and irony, the story leads us to expect or imagine an action climax: Almeida delivering some crushing verbal indictment to her cousin's face, or maybe even a crushing boot to her backside. Almeida encourages us to expect this climax because she would like to do it, recognizes the sweet moment it would give her. But of course, given that this is a story with fidelity, from the point of view of a grieving but reasonable person, she does not. The line we have all heard before ("It was so good of you to come") emerges from Almeida, and that little irony is what stands in the place of some other story's sword fight. It is the epiphany.

"Visitation" also proves that humour and tragedy are, or can be, fictionally compatible. But I'll return to the story for that purpose in a chapter about humour.

Stories that have only rising action and suspense tend not to be found in modern short fiction. They are more likely found on TV. In television drama, the emphasis is on plot, who catches whom, who gets the money, with reasons thrown in for motivation. The better the TV show, the more meaningful the characterization that occurs within the plot.

Literary short stories tend to be like "The Dog in the Van," where the rising action combines with a powerful emotional, psychological turmoil that is the real story. Or they are stories like "Visitation" that have an increasing tension or discomfort or inner turmoil, rather than rising action, where the progress of the story is more psychological than active.

✦ ✦ ✦ Short Story Development

Two kinds of development in a short story are *rising action* and *progression toward a new understanding*.

RISING ACTION is action taken to solve a problem. Action rises because obstacles are encountered and the protagonist may fail. For example, bugs that were only in the basement are suddenly in the pantry. A time limit helps to make the action rise: act fast before the bugs infect the children.

PROGRESSION TOWARD A NEW UNDERSTANDING involves the psychology of characters the story is bringing into conflict. The characters jostle one another and against outside forces. They are pushed toward realizations, changes, unburdenings, dead ends, breakthroughs.

Before leaving the subject, I will try, briefly, to answer the question I am most frequently asked about structure: *Does it really help a fiction writer to know any or all of these things about how dramatic structure works?*

The truth is that none of the writers I know, including myself, get out their protractors at the beginning of writing a story and start defining and graphing a structure on which to slap them down. On the other hand, I believe that our knowing how stories are built by others, and our discovery of the shapes of experience that authors put fictional characters through, is important to our ability to write fiction. It may not be that important for writing the compulsive, instinctual first draft, when writers often try to forget what they're doing rather than remember it better. But later, when you are trying to improve the first draft, trying to diagnose its flaws and to rebuild it to some conclusion that feels satisfyingly like an ending, an understanding of how fiction is structured does help. For example, it can help you discover flat spots where there is no powerful reason for the reader to go on. If the highest point of action is on page two of ten, you may have built a story that disappoints rather than entices. And so on.

Though it's not something I would know how to be prescriptive about, I also believe that a better understanding of the structure of fiction can also help in the trancelike writing of the first draft, when the writer is looking for the story as much as writing it. It probably is better that we don't think about structure then. It would break the spell. But that doesn't stop the process from being silently informed by what we know.

As our understanding of fiction improves, as the number of fictional structures we know enlarges, we come to the act of writing fiction better trained, better equipped. There is more for our subconscious to draw on, which is my argument for understanding structure and narration and all the other elements that combine in the craft of fiction—and recognizing not just how they work in the writing but what effect they produce in the reading.

✦ ✦ ✦ Your Process

+ It's time to move from reading to writing—or at least to planning. Think up three ideas for short stories: a story that adheres to the traditional dramatic arc (rising action); a story that leads to an "epiphany" (progression to a new understanding); and a story that you would like to both write and read that does not rely on either structural device. Write down the story ideas in no more than a paragraph. Make sure in the first two that the problem is clearly stated and that the climax and epiphany relate back to the problem.

+ The next chapter deals with character: the power of character to shape story, and the techniques used by authors to convey and build fictional characters. As preparation, read Edna Alford's short story "Half-Past Eight."

...Half-Past Eight

a short story by **EDNA ALFORD**

     Tessie Bishop took her tube of "Scarlet Fire" lipstick and removed the lid. The lipstick was old and stale and had that sickly sweet smell peculiar to the cosmetics of the aged.

     The mirror on the dowager dresser was adjustable, swung on ornate brass hooks, and Tessie tilted it so she could see as much of herself as possible. She wished she had a full-length mirror like the one she had hung on the bathroom door of the apartment she lived in before she had to come to the lodge, before the money ran out and the time with it. She wanted to check the hem of her dress, get the overall effect of the outfit she was wearing to the Stampede Parade.

     The mirror on this dresser was tarnished and wavy—like all the others in the lodge, Tessie supposed. Her image was distorted in this mirror, unreal in the bronze shimmer. She couldn't believe she really looked like this, her skin old and wavy and discoloured, mapped with cracks. But what could you expect, she thought. Time passes, doesn't it, and all things considered, she had held her own, didn't look nearly as old as she was, she assured herself, in spite of the mirror.

Mirrors weren't trustworthy, regardless of the fairytales. "Mirror, mirror on the wall, who is the *oldest* of us all?" she mocked the white-haired woman trapped in the yellow glass. Then laughing she said, "See, you can't tell, you silly old bitch. You don't know a goddamn thing—and in a few minutes you'll know even less."

She stretched her lips thin, into a false smile. Then she slowly, meticulously spread a thick, bleeding layer of lipstick horizontally across her mouth, right to the tapered corners—first on the top lip, then on the bottom. She replaced the lid on the tube and laid it on the dresser top. She took a piece of Kleenex and patted her mouth several times, gingerly.

Next she took a round clear plastic container from a small top drawer of her dresser. The brown-stained label on the bottom read "Pomegranate Blush." She unscrewed the lid and dipped the tip of her right index finger into it. Then she smeared a round high blotch of "Pomegranate Blush" on each cheek.

The rouge was pink and had the same sweet sickening odour as the lipstick, like rosewater and glycerin gone rancid in sun and age. The bright pink cheeks clashed violently with her "Scarlet Fire" lips and together with white, heavily powdered skin in wrinkles, made her look like a clown.

She applied eyebrow pencil in thin black arches over her almost browless eyes and in conclusion, brushed mascara thickly on her short white lashes. It dried lumpy.

When she had finished, she smiled with satisfaction at the mirror. She began to hum to herself. She went to the long window of her small dark room and was delighted to see the summer sun already climbing high and hot in the eastern sky. There were only a few roguish tufts of cloud drifting easily through the blue whiteness.

She had been hoping for weeks now that there would be no rain today. She and Flora Henderson had crossed their fingers in unison yesterday—at the supper table, in the tea room, and at prayer meetings when everyone else was singing "Rock of ages cleft for me, let me hide—" they would both look out at the sky, then back at each other, hoping the weather would hold for the parade.

The weatherman on CFCN Radio last night had reported that a fine day *was* expected for the parade, that there were clouds moving in over the Rockies but they weren't expected to reach Calgary till late tomorrow. Tessie put her face close to the warm green shimmer of the window screen and breathed a satisfied, and at the same time, excited sigh of relief.

She had on her best summer dress, a flowered cotton print with huge pink and red and orange mums with black stems and leaves frolicking all over it. A thin black patent leather belt sat squarely on her hips. A very classy number, she thought. A perfect dress for a parade. She wore a navy straw hat with a small brim and last week she had bought an orange chiffon scarf to lace through the brass holes in the hat and tie pertly under her chin. The scarf perfectly matched the orange mums in the dress print.

When she brushed her hair, she flipped a small white curl on either side of her face to fall sultry against her cheeks. Her hair looked exactly as she had worn it in what she called her "hey-day," in the early twenties. Tessie had been one of the first to bob her hair and she wore it now in the same short-cropped style. Admiring herself in the wavy mirror, she remembered that she had been a very beautiful young woman. Everyone had told her so and she herself had thought that it was true.

When she was finished putting on her make-up, she put the lipstick along with her comb, some Kleenex, and her clutch purse in a small black bag she had crocheted.

Although she could barely make ends meet on the small pension she got from the Veteran's Affairs Department, she had managed to save a little over twenty dollars for today. It hadn't been easy but she had cut down on wool for crocheting last month and she made do with the meals at the lodge which, she thought, was a sacrifice, to say the least. And she hadn't bought a drop of liquor in all that time.

One good thing about today was that she didn't have to worry about Flora. Flora was game to go and always had lots of money. In fact, she was more excited about the parade than Tessie, could talk of nothing else. You'd never know she was eighty-six. Nothing could keep her down—a lot like me, thought Tessie. Age meant nothing to her, which was probably why they chummed around together, not because of the drinking, which was the opinion of most of the old biddies who lived here. And Flora always paid her own way.

There were all sorts of rumours about Flora. Some said she won the "Pot of Gold" at the fair one year and that was why she could stick her old age pension cheques under her mattress and not worry about cashing them. But Tessie knew that Flora and old man Henderson had owned a hotel up north in British Columbia and that they had catered to the men from the logging camps. Flora spent a good deal of her time supervising the girls on the top floor. "There was good money in them girls," Flora told Tessie confidentially.

Today's the day, all right, Tessie thought. Today we'll go out and see the parade and eat and kick up our heels for a change.

Leaving her bed unmade, she picked up her straw sun hat, her black bag, and a sweater just in case. She locked the door, trying the lock afterward and then walked down the hall and knocked on Flora's door, number twenty-three. She frowned down at her brown oxfords which were not beautiful and didn't match her dress. But they were sturdy, she thought, for all the walking they would have to do today.

Flora opened the door a crack. Then, finding it was Tessie, she flung the door back against the jamb. "Yah, come on in," she bellowed.

Flora, too, had high rouge blotches on her cheeks and her hair stuck pin-curl fuzzy out from under a wide-brimmed mannish straw hat. For all her money, thought Tessie, Flora might at least buy a new summer hat. That one, Tessie was sure, must have been old man Henderson's fifty years ago.

Flora wore a long-sleeved, shapeless dress of grey-striped arnel her daughter-in-law had helped her pick three years ago. But she had new shoes, handsome sturdy white sandals. Tessie felt a slight twinge when she saw them.

"Good day for a parade, eh Flora?" she said. She was not about to let on to Flora how envious she was of the new sandals.

"Good day for a parade, eh Tess?" Flora hadn't heard Tessie speak. That was another thing that irked her about the older woman. She was partially deaf. But at least she wasn't afraid to go. So Tessie smiled patronizingly at Flora. I may not have fancy sandals, she thought to herself, but at least I'm not deaf—yet.

Flora smiled back, picked up her purse and sweater, and they left the room, Flora locking the door of room twenty-three behind them. She tried the lock twice.

They passed several ancient ladies with canes, shuffle-feeling thick routes along the walls of the hallway on their way to breakfast. The hoyer stood in the middle of the lower hallway outside Miss Bole's room and Tessie edged her way around it as if she were afraid it were alive, as if it might reach out and grab her. But Flora stuck out her foot and gave the hoyer a shove and sent it rolling into the wall, clanking when it hit the baseboard, its canvas straps swinging foolishly.

"You'll never get me inta that goddamn thing," she bellered at the metal hoist used to transport bedridden lodgers to and from the bathtub. "Goddamn stupid nurse," Flora continued, "leaving that contraption out in the hall so's one of us'll fall and break our bloody hips. No more of a nurse than a pig's foot," she yelled. "She hasn't got the brains she was born with. I wouldn't hire her if ya paid me, Tess."

Tessie raised her eyebrows and smiled. Flora guffawed. "Oh Christ, Tess. She ain't fit for that kinda work!" Tessie giggled.

At breakfast Tessie and Flora had to sit with Mrs. Morrison and Mrs. Popovich because there were no spaces left at the other tables by the time they got there. Tessie had hated Helen Popovich ever since the fight over the big brown rocker on the sun porch. Tessie had lost that one, but only because Helen Popovich called in the matrons. And Mrs. Morrison wasn't much better—"Yes Helen this" and "Yes Helen that"—a spineless old bat if ever there was one.

But she tried to ignore the other two women and she and Flora talked about their plans. Would they take the bus as far as the stadium or would they walk while it was still cool? Better take the bus, they decided. No sense risking being late and missing the Parade Marshall. Tessie would definitely be upset if she missed Prince Charles.

Mrs. Popovich's forehead furrowed cynically. "Why you'd want to fight them crowds is beyond me," she clipped the remnants of a fractured voice, "and on a day like this! Good Lord, Flora, you'll shrivel up in the heat. What if you have an attack? Things aren't like they used to be you know. Nobody'll pick you up from the street now—they just leave you lying there. I know an old woman who lay for five hours, I say, on the street and her leg was broke and nobody helped her. She died too."

"We all do," Flora interrupted, "but Tessie and me ain't dead yet." She winked at Tessie and Tessie winked back.

"We won't strain ourselves, Helen," Tessie compromised. "We're just going to have a look. We don't plan to be gone long. After all, we're not going to be on the street you know. We do have seats in Mewata Stadium and we do have our hats."

"Suit yourself," Helen clucked with finality. She didn't speak to them again but when Tessie and Flora gathered their things together and strutted out of the dining room, Tessie whispered loudly, not only for Flora but so Helen could hear.

"You know what they say, Flora—mind your own business, eat your own fish—not to mention the dog in the manger." She looked around to make certain Helen had heard her and smiled with satisfaction. Helen was staring furiously at the porridge in the thick porcelain bowl on her plate. She was jabbing it viciously with the wrong end of her spoon.

Outside the building and walking on the sidewalk toward the bus stop, Tessie and Flora were a peculiar and somewhat amusing couple. Flora, although eighty-six, was still tall and raw-boned, her heavy body lumbering like a large grey-striped animal from side to side with each step. Tessie, on the other hand, was a little like a bird, very small and colourful beside Flora. The steps Tessie took were Lilliputian and energetic which produced a kind of hopping effect as she dodged Flora's large body, like a bright pecking bird on the back of a hippo.

When they boarded the bus it was already packed with an uproar of parade people. Tessie and Flora had to cling desperately to the chrome rods along the top of the seats because there was no place to sit. They didn't mind, except when the teeming vehicle lurched.

"Take it easy you old sonuvabitch," Flora called up to the driver, although he couldn't have been a day over fifty, Tessie thought, and not half-bad looking. To Tessie's embarrassment, Flora continued heckling, "I been in bloody buckboards made better time than this and was smoother too, yah, you bet—they give a better ride!" Some of the passengers nearest them giggled or muffled their laughter but one man laughed right out loud.

"What the hell's the matter with *you*?" Flora turned on him. "Ya drunk or just off your rocker?" The man laughed again and so did Flora this time.

Tessie inspected the clothing worn by the other passengers, mentally rated the parade outfits on a scale of one to ten. A zero, she thought, that one is definitely a zero. Pausing tentatively, her eyes scanned a young girl from the waist down. "If I had legs like that," she said to Flora, "I wouldn't be caught dead in shorts, even if I was sixteen-years-old."

"Yah, you bet," said Flora, "she'd be scrubbin' floors in my place." She winked at Tessie. "Not like you Tess," she added. Tessie blushed and cupped her hand over her eyes, pretending to look out the window to see where they were.

The ride to the stadium wasn't long but when they slowly and awkwardly disembarked all the while jostled and shoved by the swarming young, the two old women were relieved to breathe more deeply, even though the air was full of exhaust from the back of the bus. By now the near-noon sun was very high and the heat wafted around the women. But instead of making them sluggish or uncomfortable as it did most old folk, the heat only served to increase their excitement. Along the way to their seats, Flora openly rebuked the rude, both drivers and pedestrians. She broke a ten-dollar bill to buy them two revels and two paper cups full of Orange Crush. "Why don't you watch where you're goin', ya dirty bugger," she cursed when a young man bumped her elbow, making her spill the drinks so that her hands were sticky when they arrived at their seats.

From where they sat they could see the whole spread of the city centre—the Calgary Tower, a dull one-legged crane with a red crown, half-surrounded on one side by tall lean office buildings, the head offices of banks and oil companies, like confident prehistoric monsters with thousands of glass eyes glittering in the high hot sunlight. For a while they both stared at it, intently, as if their city were a foreign country they had never set foot in—they were not afraid, but were not exactly sure what they could expect.

They were soon distracted. Tessie first heard the off-key din of horns and the tremor of drums in the air as the great parade wound its way along farther up the route. Flora, being hard of hearing, had to be told that it was very near the stadium and then they both fidgeted, straining to catch their first glimpse of the leading entourage.

Finally the Parade Marshall rode into view. He was none other than Prince Charles himself, the Crown Prince of England. He was mounted on one of the magnificent dark R.C.M.P. stallions, just as his Uncle Edward had been so many years before. It didn't seem that long a time ago. Tessie tallied the years in her head. No doubt about it. Fifty. Half a century. It hardly seemed possible, but there it was.

Prince Edward was a doll and she hadn't been the only girl who thought so. And Charles was a fine looking young man, too—but just a boy really. Nevertheless, Tessie was impressed. He carried himself well, exactly the way Tessie thought the Crown Prince of England should. From the time he was a baby, Tessie had kept a scrapbook of newspaper clippings, pictures and stories about his arrivals and departures all over the Commonwealth. That was how she learned he was going to lead the parade. There had been big spreads about him in the newspapers, both the *Herald* and the *Albertan*, several weeks before.

Tessie was more than impressed. Other than Edward, there had been only one Marshall who had excited her more and that was Bing Crosby. He rode in a low, sleek convertible, but because Tessie had watched that parade from the street, she had been almost close enough to touch the man with the dreaming voice as he passed. "Where the blooo of the night / Meets the gold of the day (babababababababa) / Someone—waits for—meeee," Tessie crooned. In her memory, Bing had waved directly to her and at the very thought of it, she could feel a warm flow of blood flush her pomegranate cheeks. Flora never could get too worked up about the Royal Family and Bing Crosby seemed somehow after her time.

Behind the Crown Prince rode the Royal Canadian Mounted Police. To Tessie they looked like a flock of red birds, flag wings fluttering. There were white hats scattered all along the parade and the hats looked like white gulls on dark waves. And there was the waving of hand wings from the procession to the crowd and the wing-waving back from the white-hatted bleachers which to Tessie looked for all the world like an island of white birds in the middle of the city.

There was a wide assortment of Indians with red and yellow and white and blue beadwork. Riding and walking, they looked like beautiful and mystical doomed birds, feather headdresses swaying on their backs and feather plumes totter-waving from the tight headbands.

Among them walked a riderless horse with a sign hanging on its side. The sign identified the horse as the one Nelson Small Legs should have been riding. He was the young Indian man who had just taken his own life, Tessie remembered, the young man who couldn't go on with his battles with bureaucracies and reservations, the newscaster had said. Tessie pointed his horse out to Flora and reminded her who he was. "Yah, yah, yah, I know," Flora replied in a sad low voice.

Tessie hoped the riderless horse wouldn't dampen Flora's spirits. She always liked the Indian section of the parade best of all and looked forward to it every year. Tessie remembered their talks about the Indians in the North who sold their beaded moccasins to the loggers who came to the hotel. And Flora talked especially of a raven blue beauty who had worked in her house, on the top floor of the hotel. Tessie thought there was more to that part of the story than Flora let on by the far away look in her eyes when she spoke of the girl. Tessie had been around too. Flora didn't need to think she could pull the wool over *her* eyes.

But Flora soon perked up and the two old women quickly became intoxicated with the colour of the parade and the sound and with the smell of fresh horse droppings randomly and indiscreetly released by the great beasts on the pavement. The hot sun ricocheted off the trumpets and the cymbals of the strutting bands and off the majorettes' batons thrown high and gleaming into the summer sky.

Floats of paper flowers glided miraculously by themselves, dream-like, their tractors hidden under more paper flowers. Flora and Tessie both disagreed with the choice of the judges as to which floats should win the first and second prizes and they argued with each other about the way it should have been.

They drank the spectacle whole and undiluted while the sun played on their gleaming wrinkles which collected small droplets of sweat in the heat. Tessie's mascara ran and blackened the already prominent bags of skin under her eyes.

Long after the last float had passed the stadium, they sat watching the crowd clear, watching the parade trail away along the route. They were sorry it was over and only after a cleaner arrived pushing his long-handled bristle broom down their aisle, did they stand laboriously and gather their things. They started down one of the aisles of the bleachers. There were only a few people wearing white stetsons left, picking up thermoses, cushions and left-over lunches.

When they got down to the street Flora said her tongue was stuck to the roof of her mouth—that's how thirsty she was. And Tessie agreed. "You have to take it easy when you get to be our age, Flora," she said, "dehydration, you have to be careful of dehydration at our age." Flora looked shocked. "I *mean*, Flora, that we old folks need a lot of rest—and liquids—say at the Palliser Hotel, for example."

Flora laughed. "Yah, you bet, Tess. This here Rimrock Lounge—now that's what I call a nice quiet place. We should have brought the other old dames with us, Tess. Be good for 'em." Tessie hailed a Yellow Cab and they set off toward the city centre.

In the old days, Tessie remembered, the Palliser had been the tallest, most impressive building in the city, a testimonial to the indisputable might of the Canadian Pacific Railroad. But in recent years it had been dwarfed by a six-hundred-foot concrete tower which hovered over it, and by the sleek new shopping complex which appeared to be nudging the old hotel slowly toward the curb, toward the subway. She remembered when the tower had been built by the Husky Oil Company. At first it was called the Husky Tower but they had already renamed it the Calgary Tower. Why, Tessie didn't have the faintest idea, but they had done it, down in City Hall she supposed. Anyway the tower looked to Tessie like a man's you know what and she couldn't resist telling Flora that it was the biggest one she'd ever seen—and she had seen a few in her time.

The heat was beginning to work on the women as they climbed and their feet grew heavy and slow. Inside, the hotel was large and cool and bright. An enormous old chandelier glittered with amber light near the high ceiling of the lobby. The two women went directly to the Rimrock Lounge and sat down in luxuriously upholstered red velvet chairs at a small round table. Tessie ordered a Shanghai Sling with a red maraschino cherry and a piece of pineapple on top and Flora ordered a shot of whiskey, straight.

After their second drink an old man in a brown straw cowboy hat, a western tie and a big belt with a large brass horsehead buckle came over to Flora and Tessie's table. The ladies were boisterous by now and asked him to join them. He swept his cowboy hat off his head, harlequin-tipped it to the ladies and introduced himself as Hank. Hank had a lumpy hooked nose like the warted beak of an old hawk. He bought two rounds and Tessie, especially, was grateful.

"Well wha' did you ladies think of it this year?" asked Hank.

"Stacks up, I'd say," said Tessie. "Better than last year's if you ask me."

"Didya ever see so much *horseshit* in all yer life?" Hank shook his heavy hawk head.

"*Never*," Tessie replied, emphatically.

"Seems to me it don't all come from a horse's ass neither," Hank continued. "Every bloody politician in the city was there and some come all the way from Ottawa to ride over the turds—" he paused. "On second thought," he said, "maybe some of it *do* come from a horse's ass."

Tessie covered her mouth with her hand and laughed till her face turned red. Flora just threw her head back and let the laughter roll up from her belly. Her hat fell off and landed on the carpet behind her chair. Satisfied with the effect his commentary had on his new companions, Hank stretched out his legs and clasped his gnarled brown hands behind his head, slowly lifted one enormous, scuffed Texas boot and crossed it deliberately over the other boot.

"I'll tell you what I like," he drawled. "I like them majorettes with their baa-tons."

"You mean you like their legs don't you, Hank?" Tessie volleyed.

"Yah, you bet," said Flora who had her hand cupped to her best ear and had caught the word "legs.""Not too bad, not too bad at all. You and me, Tess, if we had a couple of them peaches, we could buy and sell that Pine Mountain hole ten times over. Get ourselves a fair-sized house, one of them old fellas across from Maunley Park. We'd live on the first floor and set up shop on the second. Whadaya say, Tess?" Flora's voice, low and hoarse, rumbled along like an old train.

"Why *not* Pine Mountain?" snickered Tessie. The "not" was high-pitched, a little girl's squeal. She put her hand on Hank's arm and said, "That's where we live, Hank, in the lodge," and turning to Flora, continued, "God knows it's old enough—lots of rooms. You and I could live in the Maunley Mansion, Flora, in style, like the matrons."

"Yah, you bet. Be nice and quiet. The girls could take the fellas out inta the park, under the trees—be nice in the spring, eh Tess?" She winked at Tessie and Tessie winked back.

"One small problem," said Tessie, "what do we do with all those old ladies? As you would say, Flora, they sure as hell ain't fit for work."

"Yah, you bet," Flora laughed, " as far as I can figure half of 'em don't even know where they are. Seems to me things could go on pretty much as usual, Tess, and nobody'd know the difference—but for the matrons, I guess. We might have a little trouble bringing them around."

Hank, who had finally come to appreciate the nature of Tessie's and Flora's plan, rolled his eyes toward the ceiling, then bowed his head and, tipping his hat low over his brow, drawled, 'Ah-haa—I didn't know you was that sort of ladies." Then he raised his head and stared directly at Tessie who blushed and looked down at her drink. Gingerly, she slid the maraschino cherry from its plastic green arrow and popped it into her mouth. It was sweet, deliciously sweet.

Late in the afternoon the three tottered into the hotel dining room and ordered steak sandwiches. Tessie ate too much and had stabbing gas pains for some time after the meal. Flora had trouble chewing the meat with her false teeth but she enjoyed the blood beef flavour and ate everything on her plate.

When they finished their meal the three went back to the bar. Flora had to stop at the washroom on the way. There was a line-up and Hank and Tessie could hear Flora cursing from all the way across the lobby. Once in the bar they drank beer from pitchers and sang along with a man who played a honky-tonk piano in a dark corner of the lounge. The words of the songs were projected on a white square of wall and a little ball bounced from word to word along the lyrics so they could know where they were and what to sing.

"Roll out the barrel," Flora bellowed, "we'll have a barrel of fun," not always in tune or in time with the piano.

Tessie's hands fluttered and she leaned her old body, covered in orange and pink and red mums, languorously toward Hank as they sang together and whispered ripe jokes which Flora couldn't hear but laughed at anyway.

Once, while asking "What'll the ladies have?" when buying another round, Hank slapped Tessie's thigh and left his hand on one of the large orange mums that clung to the cloth of her dress. He left it there for what seemed a very long time to Tessie and she felt the blood rise to the rouge on her cheeks. She winked at him. Flora didn't see any of this and Tessie didn't let on to her what had happened.

After awhile, Flora began to doze and snore intermittently. Twice, she nearly fell off her chair. The second time, she almost tipped the chair over and that seemed to startle her, perk her up. Tessie had to admit she was a bit disappointed in Flora for petering out so fast, but then she was so much older than Tessie.

Hank had just come back from the washroom and had poured himself another glass of beer when Tessie felt the hand on her stocking, moving up her thigh. She leaned toward Hank, then straightened abruptly. Both of Hank's hands were occupied—a half-full glass of beer in one and a Player's cigarette in the other. She had just watched him light it. She turned on Flora.

"Jesus H. Christ, Flora!" she yelled. "That's the limit! We're going home!" She blushed. The people at the next table all turned and looked at her as if she'd lost her mind. Hank was looking at her that way too.

"Oh come on, Tess," Flora cajoled, "I didn't mean nothin' by it. The party's just beginning."

"I say it's over, Flora. Come on." Despite Hank's slurred protests, Tessie went out to the lobby and called a cab. When she came back, she picked up Flora's hat and their purses and they left. Hank walked out to the lobby with them. Before Tessie passed the doorman, she turned and pretended to look back at the glittering old chandelier. But she couldn't see Hank. He must already have gone back into the bar.

Tessie was furious with Flora, plunked the older woman's hat on her head, put her in the back seat of the cab, and climbed in the front with the driver. But after they had been driving for awhile, she began to calm down. No point in looking back, she thought to herself. She shouldn't have done it. It never worked. And there was no sense spoiling the whole day because of what Flora did, not over a little thing like that. Flora was drunk. That was the problem. But they'd gotten drunk together before and there was none of this nonsense. Must have been the parade, thought Tessie, all those bloody majorettes and all those Indians. She thought about that for a moment. Well, at least Flora would go with her, wasn't afraid of a little fun, and there was no harm done after all.

Instead, Tessie began to worry that the matrons would be up, or that the night nurse would catch them coming in. With any luck Mrs. Tittler would be asleep, but if she wasn't—. Tessie sighed deeply, then belched. Her stomach was full of gas again because of the beer. Not only that, she was pretty sure she would be hung over in the morning.

Flora began to sing in a subdued, broken voice, "Roll out the barrel, we'll have a barrel of fun—," then stopped abruptly in the middle of the first verse as if she had just remembered something vitally important. She laughed and launched into a rollicking chorus of a different song, sung to the tune of "The Dark-Town Strutters' Ball"—

OOOH—there's gonna be a ball
the mother-fuckers' ball.
The witches an' the bitches
gonna be there all.
Now honey, don't be late
'cause we'll be passin' out
pussy 'bout half-passed eight

I got fucked in France,
fucked in Spain,
I even got a little
on the coast of Maine—
but the best damn piece of all
was my goddam mother-in-law
last Saturday night
at the mother-fuckers' ball.

The cabbie tipped back the brim of his hat, looked over his shoulder and grinned. "That's a new one on me," he said. "I thought I'd heard 'em all."

"Huhaw!" Flora guffawed. "Do I look like I'd be singin' a new song?"

That wasn't very likely, Tessie thought, regarding her old friend with amusement and a fair amount of admiration, but then Tessie had never heard the song before either—and she had been around.

"Oh yah, we sung it in the bar all the time, years ago, up North in my old man's hotel." She paused, remembering. "Yah," she said quietly, "that's an old dog."

As they climbed the steps toward the dark building, Tessie could hear the roll of thunder in the black west. She smelled something dank, like mildew, in the air. That's all right, she thought. Let her come down in buckets—all night if she wants to, and all day tomorrow. As long as it didn't rain today.

At the top of the steps, Flora rattled her throat, dragged up a patch of phlegm and spat it into the flower bed beside the lodge where it hung white and bubbly on a purple petunia. Tessie winced. They snuck in through the sun porch door which, luckily, had not yet been locked. In all likelihood, Mrs. Tittler had completely forgotten about it again, Tessie thought.

In the feeble light of the porch, Tessie noticed that Flora's straw hat sat awry and saucy on her head. Someone might get up. Maybe Mrs. Tittler would come out and see the tilt and suspect. "Stand still a minute will ya, Flora," she said. She reached up and straightened the hat and fuss-tucked the fuzzy grey strands of hair under the brim. Flora pretended to stand at attention.

But no sooner had they started up the hall when Flora began to wander from one side to the other, banging on each door and roaring, "Wake up ya deaf old coots! C'mon now, outa the sack!" Then she began to sing—"Oh, there's gonna be a ball, the mother—"

"Shshshsh," Tessie pleaded, her right index finger poised dramatically stiff and vertical over her red-crusted lips. "You'll wake 'em up for shhure, you crazy old drunk!"

"What's a matter with ya, Tess?" Flora bellered to the lodge of aged sleeping ladies. "I'd rather be fuckin' drunk than this." She wheeled and staggered, raised her right arm, waved it around in the air and, fisting the fingers, resumed weaving back and forth across the hall, banging on bedroom doors and singing—

The witches an' the bitches
gonna be there all.
Now honeee, don't be late
'cause we'll be passin' out—

"Jesus Christ," she interrupted herself, "most of these old dames don't even make it to seven-thirty let alone half-past eight—and the worst of it is they wouldn't know what to do with it even if they could get holda some."

Tessie, who was now standing in the stairwell at the other end of the hall, stopped tapping her foot. Though she was half-hidden in shadow, her moon white face appeared to project itself out of the dark, like a mask on a stick. Her eyes were rimmed in black where the mascara had run in the hot afternoon sun and met the thin black arches pencilled on her brows.

● ● ●

...6

How Character Drives Story

The creation of character in fiction is so important, so central to the art, that the writer who can do it is often forgiven other weaknesses. An impression or feeling or mental image of a character is often what the reader takes away from a story and keeps longest.

Your ability to select parts of people you have known, or even just read about or passed by, to process them through your mind and come up with living, breathing, speaking fictional characters is perhaps the most creative act of all. As such, this ability might be an aspect of talent that can't be taught. What can be done—to discover and encourage your talent in this direction—is to make a conscious effort to observe people around you. Carry a notebook. Take notes. Don't let the good stuff fall out of memory. Get over the fear that people will see themselves in your characters and be offended. They will, whether they're present or not.

You can also study good fiction and define and then practise the techniques by which those writers build and enliven their characters. That is the purpose of the present chapter: to examine the methods of characterization used by Edna Alford in her story "Half-Past Eight." I'll also continue to refer to "Visitation" and "The Dog in the Van."

✦ ✦ ✦ Decision at the Crossroads: The Path Not Taken

All fiction is character driven. The unfolding of characters, the changes within characters, and particularly the decisions characters make *generate the plot of the short story or novel.*

Now, for an exercise that proves the point:

Think up a character. Don't invent one. Just select someone from your life. For the purposes of the exercise, this character must have a lover or a spouse with whom he or she lives. If the person you have in mind has no significant other, invent one or select someone else. This is what happens to your character:

> *He or she has just left home for work. The spouse was at home at that time and looked about to leave for work as well. A mile down the road, your character thinks about the iron. He or she ironed a shirt for work but can't remember if the iron was shut off afterward. You know how it is when something like that gets into your head; there's nothing for it but to go back and check. Your character rushes into the house and upstairs, and finds the spouse in bed with someone else.*

The question that only you can answer, through your knowledge of the person you have selected, is: "What happens next?"

Does your character fly into a rage, meekly depart, burst into tears, break every dish in the house, pull out an Uzi, jump in the middle, break the hood ornament off the spouse's Mercedes on the way to the travel agent?

The point of the exercise is that the range of possibility for a specific character is not the same thing as the range of possibility for all characters everywhere. Chances are your thought process is something like this: "Priscilla's pretty calm but lethal too in her way. I don't think she'd yell. I'm sure she wouldn't weep. I remember that time she went after Bill with the fireplace poker for playing that terrible practical joke, so if there was a blunt instrument available …" And so on. Whatever your character does in response to the situation is a direct outgrowth of personality.

One way to think of a story is as a series of decision points, or as a journey where the decision points are the crossroads. The decisions will be made according to character. The decision points plotted onto a map are the journey itself, and that plot has been generated out of character.

A statement you will often hear from a euphoric writer is that the story he or she is working on seems to be "writing itself."

I didn't feel I was in control at all. The story was writing itself.

Some attribute this sensation to mystical guidance, a voice speaking through them, perhaps a spirit from the other world. A more basic explanation is suggested by the exercise you've just completed. If your characters are fully drawn, if you understand them well, *they will come to life.* When a decision point arrives, their response will be there, without you as writer having to think about it. They have minds; they will make them up for themselves.

Knowing the character is also the best preparation for dialogue. They cannot *but* speak like themselves. The characters' spoken responses seem to come not from you but from them, which is exactly as it should be.

The converse is also true. If your story bogs down, doesn't seem to want to go anywhere, I always suggest that you go back to character. Probably your character is not defined and alive for you yet, and hence cannot act or speak independently. Study your characters. Get to know them better. Write monologues in their voices, not necessarily even about what your story is about. Ask your character to give his or her opinion of pro wrestling. Pose imaginary situations, again not necessarily from your story, and predict what your character will do. When your character becomes alive for you, is speaking in your mind, he or she should have the power to move the story.

Then there is the writer who works out a neat and intricate plot, and when he or she gets tucked into the writing, the story goes somewhere else, giving the writer the choice of beating the story into submission or letting the story go where it wants to go. The wise writer goes where the story wants to go, because that is where the character is taking it. If you choose the opposite and force the character to go where you had originally planned, the story will feel forever false. You cannot evolve plot and character in isolation from each other. The plot only makes sense if it is a plot the character can naturally deliver.

Before leaving the subject of how characters generate plot, let's look at how the characters Tessie and Flora create the plot of Edna Alford's "Half-Past Eight." The two women are friends. They live in a seniors' lodge in Calgary and they are about to go downtown to watch the Calgary Stampede Parade.

The two women pride themselves on being more game than the other old women at the lodge. They are risk takers; "not dead yet," as Flora puts it. To live up to their legend, they must go to the parade and then for drinks. They must stay out late.

The voice or point of view in the story belongs to Tessie, a third-person point of view, and she thinks about the two of them this way:

> *One good thing about today was that she didn't have to worry about Flora. Flora was game to go and always had lots of money. In fact, she was more excited about the parade than Tessie; she could talk of nothing else. You'd never know she was eighty-six. Nothing could keep her down—a lot like me, thought Tessie.*

Because the characters are elderly, because of their hubris, the reader feels instinctively protective of them. This impulse is one of the hooks that binds the reader into the story. When their mutual fondness for drink is mentioned, the reader fears for their safety and dignity. When another old lady warns them of the heat of the day, of the possibility of "an attack," that fear is also put in the reader's mind. But Tessie and Flora are not to be held back. The story proceeds, bargaining against the expectations Edna Alford has seeded and against the expectations we ourselves have about the elderly.

If you look for it, you will see how the characters of Tessie and Flora generate the plot every step of the way. Their willingness to take a chance, to have an adventure, gets them on the bus and to the parade in the first place. After the parade, the story hits the crossroads: go home or go for a drink? And the story is already writing itself in our heads through character, because we know they will choose the drink. It is their personality to do so, and there is also the pact between them, to not chicken out.

From the length of time Tessie took to do her makeup at the start of the story, the attention to every detail, we get the picture that she was attractive in her day, and that she has not entirely given up this vision of herself in old age. Her interest in men has also made her alert to Flora's interest in women.

When they meet Hank, these properties of character generate the next development. They have a number of drinks, and Tessie begins to flirt with Hank. She ignores Flora, who begins to slip into drunkenness and sleep. Flora, so brash to begin with, weakens and falters when she is not, or cannot be, the centre of attention. Tessie, so timid at first, is full of Dutch courage now and feeling her old capacity to tantalize a man.

Then, in the pivotal moment, a hand lands and moves on Tessie's leg. She leans toward Hank, but sees his two hands above the table, occupied with a drink and a cigarette. The hand belongs to Flora! Tessie blows up, cuts off the evening, demands that they go home.

Right to the end, character is moving the story where it goes. A little lust, a little jealousy, a lot of drinks, and Flora steps over the boundary that is ordinarily observed between them. With her personality accelerated by drink, Tessie does not respond timidly. She is forceful. She won't stand for it.

✦ ✦ ✦ Detail and Character

Most everything about fiction is conveyed through detail. The quality of fiction is often equal to the quality of the details that make it up. If you portray a setting, whether it's the towering red cliffs of Sedona or a townhouse rumpus room, the details selected and their wording affect their fidelity and impact, the ability of the good reader to see and feel it.

So too with the details by which you convey character. We probably all know from some lamentable conversation or another that it is possible to talk all day about a character and convey nothing. Often, when you ask what people look like, you get their height. "She is five feet, seven inches." Perhaps 2 per cent of the women in the world are that height. So what does this tell me? Or you'll hear someone ask, "What's he like?" The other person will answer, "He's nice." Very few people are not to some degree nice.

Nice is also not a detail. It is a generalization, and you will find that generalizations and summations are useless in fiction. They refer to a class of people or a characteristic that defines a class of people. The art of characterization in fiction deals with the individual, not the group or class. Your task is to differentiate the fictional individual from all other people, real or imagined. Sometimes, you make them specific by comparison to others, but your goal is always to make them visible and recognizable as individuals.

To accomplish this goal, you need to provide details that are specific enough, startling enough, vivid enough, that the reader can begin to construct the character you intend. Maybe the detail is so good, we get it right away.

Specific, not unique, is what is important. It is the fact that we recognize the detail from having seen it that allows the communication of a character. Someone absolutely unique in fiction might not be recognizable.

In the opening paragraphs of Edna Alford's "Half-Past Eight," Tessie is putting on her makeup. Instead of simply saying that and conveying a general impression of someone named Tessie performing that action, Alford tells us that the lipstick she applies is "Scarlet Fire" (which sounds five-and-dime already), is "stale" (implying infrequently used), and has "the sickly sweet smell peculiar to the cosmetics of the aged." (Tessie is elderly.)

If you stop right there and ask yourself what you know about Tessie, the answer is—surprisingly, considering you're three lines in—a lot. She is elderly, wears cheap red lipstick that goes stale on her, and is probably not well off. All of this knowledge is a credit to the details chosen and their wording by the author. Each detail has been a charge that explodes into meaning the second we read it.

The next two paragraphs are devoted to the mirror and what Tessie sees in it. The description of the mirror's faults as compared to the one she had in her apartment before she moved to the lodge tells us the basic moves of her recent life. It reinforces that she is elderly. It describes movement in her life from free to less free. It conveys that the nursing home is not posh, so probably neither is she.

The shock she feels at her image in the mirror, the way that she regains some of her old confidence as the makeup goes on, tells us that she considered herself pretty at one time and feels she is still holding her own, at least in comparison to the others at the lodge.

The makeup ritual goes on for two pages, and as it does, the list of things we understand about Tessie lengthens rapidly: elderly, not well off, lives in a lodge, looks-conscious, capable of vulgar outburst, and so on.

I've already talked about the need for the details to be specific and vivid. To be of any use they also have to be the right ones to convey the character. They have to be well chosen. A scattergun effect seldom works. But the details also have to be motivated, and this aspect of detail may be the most often ignored.

If you have a great detail, explosively vivid, precisely worded, and it doesn't seem to deliver the impact it should, the problem may well be that there is no reason for its being there. It may come from the writer's observations or imagination without ever having any place in the character's world.

Every detail of Tessie's makeup ritual is important to Tessie. These are the tools with which she restores the vestige of her prettiness, her one-time glamour, the part of herself she has relied on to get her through. The strength of these details in the story comes partly from the reminder that an elderly woman can be as capable of vanity as anyone else.

Someone might come along and say, "But clothes and makeup and hair don't make the woman." But Tessie believes they do. She has staked her life on it. Edna Alford lets Tessie think and act as Tessie would, whether it's politically correct or not, whether it is Edna Alford's opinion or not. She doesn't "social work" her characters or her story.

The reason good fictional details work as well as they do doesn't entirely come from the writer or the story. What the writer is doing is tapping into the reader's expertise as an observer of the world. A detail is as good as the reader who recognizes it and understands what it reveals.

✦ ✦ ✦ The Sound of the Voice in the Story

Edna Alford's fictional Tessie is also conveyed to readers through the story's voice. Voice is most obviously a tool of characterization in fiction when the story is told in the first person. In a first-person story or novel, we know we're hearing the character, and we learn his or her personality as we would by listening to anyone. Third-person narration (the choice in "Half-Past Eight") is more subtle and has more variation. At one end of the spectrum, third-person narration is first-person narration with the *I* converted to *he* or *she*. The voice is still very much the character's voice. At the other end of that third-person spectrum, third-person narration is a neutral voice, as if the story is written by one who is travelling *with* the character rather than *in* the character. Between those two end points, are any number of alternatives, all varying according to the distance between the voice and the character.

In "Half-Past Eight," the third-person narration (favouring Tessie) is mostly neutral, describing what she does and occasionally what she thinks without choosing to sound exactly like her. But at the same time, the narration does lean toward Tessie's syntactical world, her vocabulary, and her cultural self. Without speaking in her voice, it still conveys her. For example, there is probably not a word in the story that Tessie would not know or could not speak.

Nor is the narrative voice always the same distance away from her. Sometimes it leans so close it will be Tessie's voice for a sentence or two. "Flora was game to go and had lots of money." Then it will weave out to a more neutral distance. "At breakfast Tessie and Flora had to sit with Mrs. Morrison and Mrs. Popovich because there were no spaces at the other tables." Finally, at the end, Alford leaves Tessie, suddenly and shockingly, and instead of considering her appearance from within, she perceives it from across the room, as a stranger might.

Tessie, who was now standing in the stairwell at the other end of the hall, stopped tapping her foot. Though she was half-hidden in shadow, her moon white face appeared to project itself out of the dark, like a mask on a stick. Her eyes were rimmed in black where the mascara had run in the hot afternoon sun and met the thin black arches pencilled on her brows.

✦ ✦ ✦ Characterization by Description

Characterizing people by physically describing them is a natural thing to do in fiction because it is a natural thing to do in life. We do it all the time whenever our curiosity is aroused about someone. Hence, when Cousin Martha shows up at Almeida's door in "Visitation," Almeida considers what Martha looks like. She hasn't seen Martha in a long time. She is motivated to consider how Martha has stayed the same, how she has changed. This is an important method by which Martha is characterized in the short story.

This fiftyish person with her rosy cheeks, clear eyes, rounded body, had little to do with the Sapphire who'd danced in gauzy veils at the Blue Donkey. Fine, was the word for this woman. Healthy, was another. Gaudy, was another still.

It is just as natural that Dick Crossley, in "The Dog in the Van," would physically describe Larry, the owner of the dog, when he first meets him. He has been thinking throughout the story about what kind of person the dog's owner must be, so the description is motivated. Motivation is all-important. There must be a reason for a character to describe another.

What is difficult to accomplish in a story is a motivated physical description of the point-of-view character, because it demands that the character describe him or herself, and why do that? In "Half-Past Eight," Edna Alford illustrates one good method. Tessie is putting on her makeup and is confronted in the mirror by a shocking sight. She sees that she is old, and although she probably sees that every day, she happens to care more about it today because she is going to the parade. This method works because it is completely in character for Tessie to study her appearance at length. Putting on makeup requires that she do so.

Another way that authors accomplish this is through photographs and home videos. The character sees him or herself and has a motive to consider that appearance. As long as you're asking the question "Why would my character describe him/herself?" you'll probably come up with a plausible answer.

Some writers refuse to describe their characters at all, especially their point-of-view character, reasoning that it gets in the way of the reader's imagery and choices.

If motivation is the most important thing about characterization by description (why describe this person?), the next most important thing is the need to infuse the description with some emotion. No description in fiction should be presented without some emotion.

In the questions at the end of this chapter, you will find the following:

a. Describe a man.
b. Describe a man baking a cake.
c. Describe a man baking a cake when sad.
d. Describe a man baking a cake when he's sad and you're angry.

The point is to give you the means of proving to yourself that people are always doing something and that their actions are always imbued by whatever they are feeling. Your (or your character's) view of them is always coloured by emotion as well. There is simply never a reason for describing people as if they were frozen in time, or on a slab, unless they are.

Again consider "Visitation." The point of the story is that the events are imbued with Almeida's grief. She is the point-of-view character, so that everything we see, we see through that grief. Because she has a sense of humour so strong it cannot be collapsed by grief, we are viewing many things through a combination of humour and grief. The characterization of Martha is often amusing. But imagine a parallel story where Martha comes to visit Almeida two weeks before the death of Almeida's daughter. You can imagine that the humour would still be there, the exasperation, but the story beyond that would be entirely different in emotion. The characterization of Martha would differ according to Almeida's mood in that other story, just as Almeida's character would appear to us differently than it does in her grief.

✦ ✦ ✦ When Characters Speak

Dialogue is a major tool for breathing life into fictional characters. It is singled out in the title of this chapter partly because of its importance and partly because writers often think of it as a separate craft from characterization—often the part of the craft at which they feel most inadequate.

If you doubt the ability of dialogue to define or redefine your sense of a character, consider how often you've heard people say, "He looked great until he opened his mouth." Every day we perceive character through what people say. When you use dialogue to portray your character, you're again tapping into a precise and well-honed skill on the part of readers.

It is impossible to say what good dialogue is and isn't in the abstract because it is entirely an outgrowth of character. If I said good dialogue consists of short pithy exchanges, I would deny the fictional existence of all characters whose nature is to speak at length. It is a matter of culture and personality how long a person comfortably or traditionally speaks. Some cannot speak at length, and it would be ridiculous to force them to. I remember a Midwestern American author lamenting that his fictional milieu was not in the deep south of Tennessee Williams. That is, the author could imagine wonderful long and eloquent speeches which the culture of his characters would not permit.

What is valuable in dialogue, and what makes dialogue so powerful at conveying character, is fidelity and consistency: finding how a particular character sounds and writing that person's dialogue so that the sound and the other individual flourishes are there. One way of testing dialogue at the editing stage is to run a character's dialogue lines together and read them aloud. Or have someone read the block of dialogue statements to you. Do they seem to originate from the same person? Which ones stick out? A sharp criticism I have heard of a few of our literary lions is that you can't tell their characters apart in dialogue. There may be rare cases where the cultural imprint of speech is so strong that most people do sound alike within that tribal context, but generally too much similarity would be a flaw. When David Adams Richards, for example, writes of the Mirimachi, he manages to come up with characters who are linked by their culture and poverty (things that make them sound similar), but have their own personalities, speeds, habits, and quirks (things that make them sound unique).

Edna Alford has wonderful dialogue in "Half-Past Eight." When Flora is singing her dirty song in the cab, and the cab driver is trying to humour her, he says the song is a new one on him. Flora guffaws and says, "Do I look like I'd be singin' a new song?" Study how Edna Alford differentiates the dialogue of the two women. Tessie is more precise and conservative. Flora is coarse, fierce, and antagonistic, more inclined to flavour her speech with shocking words and phrases. Think of how Tessie's speech is different when she's talking to Flora and when she's talking to Hank in the bar.

Something to look out for—a potential flaw, like lack of consistency—is going too far in an attempt to reproduce speech fidelity. This is most obvious in those who try to precisely represent dialect. Fictional speech faithfully presented with apostrophes inside words and dropped *g*'s and dropped *h*'s, phonetic spellings, is so hard to read the reader hears nothing. Writers who present dialogue in this way forget that the ability of readers to hear speech while reading at a normal pace is the key to success. If readers have to stop and sound out every word or phrase, they are hardly experiencing the scene as a flowing dialogue. Samuel Selvon, the great Trinidadian-Canadian writer (*The Lonely Londoners, Moses Migrating*), had a knack of conveying Caribbean dialogue that you could hear without struggle. Asked if it was the way people spoke in Trinidad, he said, "Of course not. That would not be understandable."

And that is the point about dialogue. Fictional dialogue is not the same as real conversation, and woe to the writer who tries to make it so. The fidelity we seek in dialogue is always an illusion. If you're in any doubt about this point, record a conversation and transcribe it. Without the body language, the eye contact, the context, and shared touchstones, transcribed dialogue makes little sense. What we do as fiction writers is create a simulation that has enough values of speech so that it is accepted as speech.

Another pitfall of fiction is to write out everything your character has to say even if it isn't interesting. If Uncle Billy is prone to long stories, don't present one in its entirety. Use a trick like this one: "So Phyllis, having endured Uncle's stories before, got into a comfortable position. This story featured a grumpy billy-goat and a travelling salesman."

Ascribing the dialogue (that is, telling who is speaking) is also an important matter of craft. Some writers feel compelled to find alternatives for "he said" and "she said."

"Oh damn," she hissed. (Beware of having people hiss things that aren't sibilant.)

"I'm not taking it anymore!" he screamed.

"Delightful," they snorted in unison.

I strongly advise you not to do any of this. Stick with "he said" and "she said," or you can produce unintentional comedy or the look of an amateur.

Hand in hand with this is the use of adverbs to qualify the speaking verb.

"You are the love my life," he mumbled soulfully.

"That's impossible," she snorted derisively.

Don't do this either. I am not a fan of adverbs. I often find them a redundant part of speech. In dialogue, they're especially so. We read dialogue, perhaps hear it in our brains; then the author tells us how it was spoken, with what quality. Are we supposed to go back and mumble it soulfully, snort it derisively? It makes no sense.

✦ ✦ ✦ Other Ways of Breathing Life into Characters

Beyond the voice of a character, the description of a character, and the spoken dialogue of a character, many more techniques for characterization in fiction are worth using. You are told as a fiction writer to show and not to tell so often that the advice blurs into nothing. But it is still good advice. Showing a character in action is a fine characterization technique. A tendency of some writers is to have their characters do nothing, to be minds on sticks. They move from chair to couch to bed and back to chair. It is good to remember that there are people out there who do not think at length or speak at length, and who can only be characterized by what they do.

Another characterization method that avoids the overuse of inner monologues, or improbably revealing conversations, is to describe where a character lives or works, or to describe the person's car. We are in a way what we own, and how we care for what we own. It may not be a reliable indicator of personality to say that a person owns an electric footbath, but it does say something, as does a stamp collection or bare walls.

> *I couldn't understand for a while what I found so unsettling about his apartment. Finally, I realized that while it had normal enough clutter between the walls, it had nothing on the walls—not a single thing.*

Items present or absent are good clues to character. Remember as well that readers like to participate in the analysis of these clues. When you describe a character's physical possessions or dwelling, don't always feel that you have to analyze every bit of it before the reader has a chance to think what it might mean.

Another underused characterization technique is the reactions that people have to a character. I always like it when a character who's a little too likeable is detested by a dog or a cat or a child. It's one of those non-specific indictments that might mean something and might mean nothing, and which the character cannot control. The character can't go to the cat and say, "I see you feel a little reluctant about me, but I assure you I'm a golden fellow." Fiction is not a court of law. There are few rules of evidence. "Where there is smoke, there is fire" may not be legally fair, but it is fictionally fair.

I'm also a fan of the "unreliable narrator," who gives you a version of people and events that turns out not to be true, in whole or in part. The arrival of a character who knows something contradictory is a great device for revealing that unreliability.

People say they read fiction for plot, and I don't necessarily disbelieve them. But even in the genres of fiction most known for their plots—science fiction, mystery, espionage—the books with the strongest characterizations tend to be the most popular and enduring. Among the writers of the spy novel, for example, John Le Carré reigns supreme. It is probably not a coincidence that his George Smiley is one of the most fully drawn, believable, and well-remembered characters in modern fiction.

✦ As promised:
   a. Describe a man (three sentences);
   b. Describe the same man baking a cake;
   c. Describe the same man baking a cake when sad;
   d. Describe the same man baking a cake when he's sad and you're angry.

✦ Generate three fictional characters to serve as point-of-view characters in a short story. Write paragraphs about the characters that illustrate what they're like.

✦ In a previous exercise, you came up with three story ideas. Try to imagine each of your three characters (from Question 2) as the point-of-view character in each of these three plots. (Don't worry if they won't work. This exercise often shows that the characters of a story and the idea of a story should evolve together.)

✦ Take one of the story ideas—the one you are most driven to work on—and devise a character for it who you imagine will carry the idea where you want it to go. Write an opening page for that story from the point of view of the character you imagine.

✦ Read Diane Schoemperlen's "Stranger Than Fiction" as a preparation for the deeper discussion of point of view in the next chapter.

···*Stranger Than Fiction*

a short story by **DIANE SCHOEMPERLEN**

Any number of people will tell you that truth is stranger than fiction. They will usually tell you this as a preface to the story of how their Aunt Maude was frightened by a bald albino juggler at the East Azilda Fall Fair when she was six months pregnant (the juggler, himself frightened by a disoriented cow that had wandered into the ring, lost control of five airborne bowling pins, and one of them hit poor old Maude square in the back of the head) and later she gave birth to a bald brown-eyed baby, Donalda, who was allergic to milk and her hair grew in so blonde it looked white and now she's unhappily married to a man who owns a bowling alley in downtown Orlando.

Or they will tell it to you as an afterword to the story of how Rita Moreno appeared to their best friend, Leona's, first cousin, Fritz, in a dream, doing the Chiquita Banana routine and feeding the fruit off her hat to a donkey, and sure enough, the next day, Fritz, who was an unemployed actor, got his big TV break doing a commercial for Fruit of the Loom underwear and he was the grapes.

Oh sure, lots of people will tell you, and with very little provocation too, that truth is stranger than fiction. But I, now I have got *the proof*.

I was writing a story about a woman named Sheila. Apropos of nothing, the name Sheila, I discovered, is an Irish form of Cecilia, from the Latin, meaning "blind". In the story, Sheila was thirty-two years old, slim, attractive, and intelligent with blue eyes and straight blonde waist-length hair. (I often give my fictional characters blue eyes and blonde hair because I have brown eyes and brown hair and I don't want anyone to think my work is autobiographical. Also, my hair is naturally curly, short.)

Sheila was married to a handsome brown-haired man name Roger, a bank manager, and they lived in a ranch-style bungalow in Tuxedo Park. Sheila amused herself by taking aerobics one afternoon a week, doing volunteer work at the senior citizens' home, and having long lunches a lot with her friends. She and Roger got along well enough, although every once in a while Sheila would remember that they hadn't had a meaningful conversation in four years. They lived an easy life, gliding gracefully and politely around each other like ice dancers.

So then I made Sheila unhappy in her heart of hearts: because what's a good story without a little angst?

The thing was, Sheila wanted to be someone else. Sheila wanted to be a country and western singer. She knew all the words to all the best songs, which she practised by singing along with the CD player while Roger was away all day at the bank. She had a special secret wardrobe stashed in the back of her walk-in closet off the master bedroom. On the cover of her first album, she wanted to see a picture of herself astride a white horse in her chaps in the wind. Having never been much bothered by either self-doubt or self-examination, it did not even occur to her that she might very well be crazy or untalented.

Then she met a man named Carlos in a specialty record store called Country Cousins. Carlos bore a startling resemblance to Johnny Cash in his younger days. Of course they hit it off right away because they were both looking for that old Patsy Cline album with "I Fall To Pieces" on it. They went out for a beer at The Hitching Post, a nearby country bar where, as it turned out, Carlos's band, The Red Rock Ramblers, was playing. They were only in town for the week, having just spent two months on the road, and now they were heading home to Saskatoon. Feeling gently homesick, Carlos talked a lot about the prairies, which Sheila had never seen, about the way they'll change colour in a thunderstorm or a dangerous wind, the way they'll make you think of things you've never thought before because you can see them forever and they have no limits. So by the time he got around to also telling her he had a wife and three kids out there, it was too late to turn back now, because he already had his hand on her thigh and his tongue in her ear.

I was having a bit of a time of it in my own life right then. Three and a half weeks earlier I had fallen in love with a man name Nathan who was from Winnipeg and also married. This was in July and it was hot, humid, and hazy; it was hard to concentrate. I was downtown Friday night having a drink at The Red Herring, which is an outdoor patio bar with a magnolia tree, orange poppies, handsome waiters, and blue metal tables sprouting red and white umbrellas advertising Alfa Romeo, Noilly Prat, and OV. The regular clientele consists largely of writers, painters, and jazz piano players who are just taking a little break in the sun. Nobody ever really gets drunk at The Red Herring: they just relax, recharge, have pleasant informed conversations about postmodernism, Chinese astrology, and free trade. They are intense and innocent.

Nathan was drinking alone and so was I, leaning against the stand-up bar inside. I'm not even sure how we first got talking but, lo and behold, the next thing you know, he's telling me that he's a writer too! Well, you can just imagine my joy at discovering we had the whole world in common. He wrote poetry, mind you, whereas I write fiction, but I was willing, for the most part, to overlook this minor discrepancy. He was in town for a weekend workshop at the university. He was dynamic, sensitive, intelligent, funny, clean-shaven, tall, fairly well off, very supportive, unhappy in his marriage, and he'd even read my books. So what else could I do? (Caught now in the act of recollection, I recognize how flimsy all this sounds, but at the time it was compelling.)

We found a table on the patio and drank a bottle of expensive white wine while talking about our favourite writers, books, and movies, our favourite foods, colours, and seasons, and the worst reviews our respective books had ever received. We congratulated ourselves on being so much alike and ordered another bottle of wine.

He did not talk about his wife, except to say that she wasn't fond of wine, and her name was never mentioned. (I already knew from Sheila that a married man who does not call his wife by her name is pretty well ripe for the picking.) So it was easy enough, sad to say, to keeping forgetting about her.

I forgot about her as we walked back to my house arm in arm at midnight, singing a slow country song, and he was the slide guitar. I did remember her as he undressed me in the living room, but I forgot about her again as he took me in his arms and his skin was so cool. I remembered her when he sighed in his sleep, but I forgot about her again in the morning when we had a shower, some coffee, and he read to me from *The Norton Anthology of English Literature*.

Then I read him the story of Sheila so far and he said he really loved it. I took this to mean that he loved me too.

Afterwards, he told me about his teacher one summer at a writers' workshop years ago in Edmonton and this teacher was a big influence on him, always telling him, "Life ain't art." I wasn't sure how to apply this apparent truism to my own life/work but I agreed eagerly, as if it were something I'd known all along.

It was shortly after this that Carlos in the story began to look less like Johnny Cash and more like the young George Gordon, Lord Byron. He admitted that when he retired from the music business, he might take up writing. Sheila recalled, but did not relate, the story she'd heard of a writer and a doctor chatting at a cocktail party and the doctor said, "When I retire and have nothing else to do, I think I'll take up writing," so the writer said, "That's a good idea! When I retire and having nothing else to do, I think I'll take up brain surgery."

Carlos told Sheila that everybody has a book in them somewhere just waiting to be written and Sheila wondered, briefly, where the book in her might be right now: lodged behind some major organ perhaps, her liver, her lungs? She had this recurring dull ache, sometimes in her left breast, sometimes in her right. It worried her occasionally, usually late at night, and then she would lie in bed beside Roger, feeling her breasts through her pink cotton nightie, looking for lumps, holding her breath. Roger, who, she was convinced, could have slept through Armageddon, sighed dreamily and draped his left arm straight across her breasts by accident, so that she lay there pinned and pleading with God. She had come to think of this pain as her "heartache" but now she wondered if it might just be a book trying to get out.

I told Nathan this pink cotton nightie of mine had once belonged to my mother who was dead now, of lung cancer, though she'd never smoked a day in her life. He said he understood my not liking to sleep in the nude and I was relieved, as this is a point some men get funny about, as if it were an insult to intimacy or their masculinity. I told him that I might like to write a book about my mother someday, as she had led an interesting life, and he assured me that everybody has a story worth telling and I'd have no trouble finding a market for that sort of human interest thing.

I told him how my first boyfriend had convinced himself that he would die young, tragically, in great pain, and alone. His name was Cornell and he suffered from migraines and whole days during which he could not climb out from under this escalating burden of impending doom. I felt guilty for dumping him but I could not let go of my own romantic fantasy of growing old beside my one true love and we would bring each other freshly fluffed pillows and cups of weak tea as the time drew near.

Sheila touched her breasts and felt nothing. Roger in the morning was always cheerful and animated, so she never told him about the pain and the sad certainty of something that would come to her at five in the morning when the earth shifts imperceptibly on its axis and everything changes or begins to be the same all over again. When she told this to Carlos between sets at the bar, he said how his six-year-old daughter often woke screaming from nightmares in which she was afraid of everything and then he would lie beside her all night while she sighed and foundered feverishly.

At five in the morning on Sunday, Nathan got up to catch a plane and I kissed him quietly goodbye without asking how old his children were.

I am comfortable enough with the derivative aspects of Sheila's story in relation to my own. I am accustomed by now to this habit fiction has of assuming the guise of reality. I am no longer surprised to go out one night for New York steak with baked potato (medium rare, sour cream, and bacon bits) and the next day my characters are enjoying the very same meal (well done, mind you, hold the bacon bits, yes, I'll have the cheesecake please). I no longer find it unsettling to see the woman beside me in a bookstore leafing through a paperback called *How To Live With A Schizophrenic* and when I get home, the next thing you know, there's a schizophrenic in my story and that book is really coming in handy.

So the whole time I was putting Sheila through her paces, I was also thinking, with some other side of my brain, about Nathan. I wasn't seriously expecting a letter or anything as incriminating as that. I did hope that he might get very drunk sometime and call me up in the middle of the night, begging and reciting love poems. I knew this wasn't something he ever could or would (considering his wife, his kids, the prairies, and all) do sober. This just shows you how little I wanted, how little it would have taken, how very little I was asking for.

But then again, in a different mood (more confident, more optimistic, very nearly jaunty), I was also thinking: Well, why not? Why couldn't he, after sleeping with me just that one weekend, go back to his bungalow in Winnipeg, pack up his word processor, leave his wife, his kids, the dog, and the algae-eater, and come back to me with tears in his eyes and a lump of love in his throat? I would pick him up at the airport, of course (all good romantic fantasies should incorporate at least one airport scene or maybe a bus station at midnight, or rain, high winds, a blizzard, a taxi at the very least, with a surly, silent driver and the meter running), where we would float across the mezzanine and fall into each other's well-dressed tingling arms while all around us dark-skinned foreign families wept on each other and tried to catch their luggage on that stupid whirligig.

Well? Why not?

Stranger things have happened. Which is another of those truisms that people will present you with just before they tell you about the time they picked up a hitchhiker on the highway halfway between Thunder Bay and Winnipeg and he turned out to be from Wabigoon where their friends, the Jacobsens, used to live and he didn't really know them but he'd heard of them and he'd seen the same flying saucer they'd seen in 1975, August 17, 11:38 p.m.

Many of these stranger things are duly documented in the weekly tabloids which I buy occasionally at the A&P when I think no one is noticing. I take solace from the headlines, tell them to my friends, and we all laugh, comforted to know that:

MICHAEL JACKSON WAS THE ELEPHANT MAN IN HIS
    PAST LIFE
FLEA CIRCUS GOES WILD WITH HUNGER AND
    ATTACKS TRAINER
MARRIAGE LASTS FOUR HOURS — GROOM WANTED TO
    WEAR THE WEDDING GOWN
TERRIFIED TELEPHONE OPERATER CLAIMS, MY
    HUSBAND TRAINED ROACHES TO ATTACK ME
HUBBY WHO GAVE KIDNEY TO WIFE WANTS IT BACK
    IN DIVORCE BATTLE
MEN FIGHT DUEL FOR GIRL'S LOVE WITH SAUSAGES

So yes, stranger things have happened in the past. And the future, on a good day, extends eternally with the promise of more.

About the time I got Sheila to the point in the story where she was actually going to get up on stage at The Hitching Post (Roger thought she was at a Tupperware party) and sing "I Fall To Pieces" (she had her satin shirt on, her fringed buckskin jacket, her cowboy boots, and everything), I accidentally thought of a girl named Sheila Shirley Harkness who was in my Grade Nine History class. She was not a friend of mine. In fact, I avoided her, because the one time we did have lunch together in the cafeteria, she ate half my french fries right off my plate and told me the story of how her Uncle Norman had killed himself by slamming his head in the car door. Sheila Shirley Harkness was older than the rest of us because she'd failed Grade Eight twice. Her mother was that woman who walked around the neighbourhood in her curlers and a mangy fur coat, twirling a baton, singing to herself, and waving her free hand like a flag. My mother said she should be ashamed of herself, acting like that in public, as if this bizarre behaviour were something we all secretly wanted to exhibit but we knew better.

Sheila Shirley Harkness was so fat that she had to sit in a special desk. And she smelled, although this was something we girls never discussed among ourselves because maybe we were afraid that we smelled too.

Sheila Shirley Harkness gave birth to a six-pound baby boy eight days before final exams. She was one of those girls sometimes written up in the tabloids who say they never knew they were pregnant: she thought she had something wrong with her, cancer, gas, or a blocked intestine. When the baby's head came out in the bathroom at three in the afternoon, she thought she was dying, turning inside out before her very own horrified eyes. She dropped out of school then, out of sight, and kept the baby, Brian, at home. There was surprisingly little speculation as to who the father might be. It was not unimportant; rather, it was unimaginable. Immaculate conception seemed more likely than Sheila in bed with a boy, any boy, moaning.

This first Sheila (or this *second* Sheila, according to your perspective on such matters as fact/fiction, life/lies, and the boundaries or dependencies like veils hung between them) has receded fairly fuzzily into my memory now and so was probably not quite the girl I remembered anyway, was probably less frightening, less doomed, might well be working at this very minute as a high-level executive for a major advertising firm, living in a harbourfront condo with an original Matisse in the loft, brass end tables, and a marble Jacuzzi, rather than lying around all day in her underwear (yellow or grey, the elastic shot), eating maple walnut ice cream and watching *I Love Lucy* reruns while her mother bangs her head against the wall in the basement and her illegitimate children run rampant through the neighbourhood in their dirty diapers, as we all, in the grip of our mutually hard-hearted, shiny-haired adolescence, assumed she would end up.

Either way, the first Sheila was not at all like the second, like *my* Sheila, as I had come to think of her. *My* Sheila was, among other things, friendly, cheerful, clever, clear-skinned, well-educated, long-legged, ambitious, and sweet-smelling. Her last name was Gustafson and her middle name was Mary, although neither of these names actually appeared in the story. Her parents, for the sake of simplicity, were either dead or living on Ellesmere Island and so didn't bother her much anymore.

Being a fictional character, my Sheila was not obliged to explain herself to anyone or to divulge her darkest fondest secrets to total strangers. Unlike myself (with my disarming or disturbing tendency to spill my guts, to tell the worst about myself to anyone who will listen), unlike myself (me having yet to accurately determine the difference between revealing and defending yourself), unlike myself (me having only recently figured out that most people don't tell the truth about themselves, not even *to* themselves, because they don't know it, like it, or remember it), Sheila knew when to keep her mouth shut.

Nevertheless, my Sheila started to subtly change. She started feeling sluggish all the time. She wore the same old dress three days in a row. She bought a baton. She ate two cheeseburgers, a large fries, and an order of chili and toast at one sitting in a greasy spoon in a bad neighbourhood. For a minute there, she questioned the meaning of life, if there even was one, if there even *should* be one. She sniffed her armpits in public. She was on the verge of a transformation, threatening to rewrite her whole life, not to mention the story. I was having none of this.

It is for fear of exactly this sort of thing that I try never to call my fictional characters by the names of people I have really known, even just in passing. So I tried to change her name in the middle of the story. First I tried to call her Janet, then Beth, then Brenda, Delores, and Laura.

But no. None of the new names would do.

Janet was too responsible.

Beth was too timid and kept threatening to die of scarlet fever.

Brenda was too easily satisfied.

Delores was the name of my friend, Susan's, Irish setter bitch and her hair was red.

Laura was the woman who came to demonstrate a talented but over-priced vacuum cleaner all over my living room for an hour and a half one Wednesday afternoon and she was sorry she'd never heard of me but she didn't get much time to read anymore what with this new job and her two-year-old twins, not to mention her husband, Hal, and did I know Danielle Steel personally, and when I said I didn't have $2,000 to spend on anything, let alone a stupid vacuum cleaner, she said, "Now that's funny, I thought all writers were rich."

So Sheila stayed Sheila and I struggled to keep her on the right track, would not give her permission to gain weight, pick her nose, or stay in bed with her head covered up till three in the afternoon. I would not allow her, much as she tried, to dream about babies born in bathtubs, buses, or a 747 cruising over Greenland at an altitude of 22, 000 feet. Against my better judgement, I did allow her one nightmare about her mother having joined a marching band, playing the bagpipes with a sound like a cat being squeezed, and the parade stretched from one end of the country to the other, but at the very last minute her mother turned into Tammy Wynette and everything worked out all right.

Sheila got a little surly with me sometimes but that was understandable, considering her situation, her frustration, and human nature being what it is.

One Friday afternoon, when I'd manoeuvred Sheila around to the place in her life where she either had to shit or get off the pot, I decided to go down to The Red Herring for a drink instead. Sheila had been a big hit at The Hitching Post. Carlos had professed his love and offered her a job with the band. She hadn't vacuumed the house all week and Roger hadn't even noticed. Two things remained unclear: what was Carlos going to do about his family back in Saskatoon and why was Roger so dense? Now Sheila either had to pack up her buckskin and join the band (Carlos was waiting outside in a cab with the meter running, off to the airport any minute now) or go home and cook a tuna casse-role for Roger (who was stuck in rush-hour traffic at the bridge, fuming, sweating, and listening to the stock market report on the car radio). To the naked eye, this would seem like a simple choice, but Sheila didn't know what she wanted to do and neither did I. I wanted to make her live happily ever after (if only because I thought this would bode well for Nathan and me), but happy endings have fallen out of favour these days—modern (or should I say, postmodern?) readers being what they are (that is, intelligent, discerning, and slightly cynical), they find them just too hard to believe, too much to hope for, fake. Could I really hope to convince any of *them* that stranger things have happened?

I was tense and thought a drink or two might do the trick. Going to The Red Herring in the afternoon is not like going down to, say, The Sunset Hotel, where they have table dancing, four shows a day, and the regulars, in the manner of serious drinkers, gaze deeply into their glasses of draft between mouthfuls, dredging there for answers or hope because they don't know where else to look. Some woman in gold glitter high heels and pink short-shorts is dancing by herself and the old guy in the back booth is sleeping with his head on his arms, having just wet himself or thrown up under the table.

The Red Herring, on the other hand, is a classy place, and having a drink or even two or three there in the afternoon, especially on a Friday, is an acceptable enough thing for a real writer, even a female one, to do. I imagined that as I sat there sipping, my writer's block would be hanging off me with a certain attractive, highly intelligent sheen.

I mean, what can you expect of writers anyway when they are prone to sitting around all day with their heads full of events that never happened to people who never existed while conducting conversations that never took place in carefully decorated rooms that will never be built?

Besides, it was at The Red Herring where I first met Nathan, so that was another good enough reason to go there. If I am fortunate enough to get the same table (towards the back, to the left), I can imagine that he is sitting across from me, we are drinking dry white wine and smiling, holding hands and making plans. In this fantasy, his wife is not, as you might expect, dead, confined to a sanatorium, or cheerfully giving him a divorce—she has simply vanished, vaporized, dropped of the face of the earth like rain. She might even be alive and well on another planet, having assumed a whole new identity with the papers to prove it, living out her life like a pseudonym.

So I fix my eyes on the empty chair and construct long loving conversations with Nathan, who is always wearing the same navy teeshirt and white cotton pants because that's all I ever knew him in. Sometimes I get carried away and catch myself nodding and moving my lips, smiling away to beat the band. I can only hope that the other patrons, on seeing this, take me for one of those independent strong-minded women who is always inordinately pleased with her own company. But then I remember that Ann Landers column where someone complained about always being told to smile and Ann reminded her that people who walk around smiling all the time for no reason are often followed by unsmiling men in white coats.

No such luck that day though—the only empty table was one to the right just beneath the magnolia tree. Our table was occupied by four cheerful young women in straw hats and lacy sundresses. They were eating elaborate beautiful salads and toasting the glorious day with Perrier and lime. I had no reason to resent, dislike, or envy them, but I did anyway.

I ordered a peach schnapps with orange juice which is called a Fuzzy Navel, so of course the waiter and I had a chummy little chuckle over that. Then I sat back to nurse my drink and read an article in *Harper's Magazine* called "The Credible Word" by John Berger.

At the very beginning, he said: *Today the discredit of words is very great.*

And in the middle: *A scarf may demand more space than a cloud.*

And finally: *The pages burning were like ideal pages being written.*

I took this to be a validation of sorts and flipped through the rest of the magazine feeling lighthearted, encouraged, and close to inspired. (It is, I have frequently found, much easier to feel inspired in a nice restaurant, facing up to all that good cutlery, fine china, fresh pasta, and crisp lettuce, than it is in my office, facing up finally to the typewriter and all that blank paper.)

Skimming next through the "Harper's Index", I could not help but feel secure and confirmed in the knowledge that the number of brands of bottled water sold in the United States is 535, the number of fish per day that a Vermonter may shoot in season is 10, the price of an order of sushi at Dodger Stadium is only $4.50, and the number of Soviets in Petrozavodsk who were crushed to death in liquor store lineups last year was 3.

I felt myself to be having, after all, one of those dizzying days in which everything can be connected, all ideas can be conjugated and then consumed whole, sense and significance are dropped into your lap like gifts, and the very cast and camber of the air on your cheek is meaningful.

Stranger things, yes.

I ordered another drink and an appetizer, the liver pâté and some French bread.

n the asphalt, so mutilated that no one will be able to identify me. I
e this so clearly that unconsciously I brace myself for the impact, for
of ripping metal and breaking glass, as I roll through each intersec-

mes I imagine that I am one of the poor pedestrians in the crosswalk
. I am mowed down right alongside the rest of them...
gers
g woman, Wendy, pushing baby in stroller, pulling toddler in harness,
ache and hates the way her hair looks like straw in this heat
teller, Jane, on lunch, carrying roast beef on rye with pickle and cheese
white bag while worrying about varicose veins, humming sad song
ating and hearts
an, Ed, with white cane and dog, wishing he was dead or his wife was
or his children, at least, would call
essman, Martin, with briefcase, nice teeth, green tie, has not a thought
d, no reason to suspect that anyone else has either
ger things have happened.
times I imagine that I am the driver of the car, with the radio on and
to the floor, and the bodies scatter from me like pages or petals,
d. Or then they are not bodies at all but balloons, of all colours, full of
words, and hot air, bobbing up and away, bouncing off asphalt, the
the pain, and a cloud.

• • •

I eavesdropped intermittently on the couple at the next table who were
talking about their old dog, Shep, who was going blind, poor thing, about their
new vacuum cleaner, and a misguided woman named Lisa who was looking for
trouble and she was sure going to get it this time, couldn't she see that guy was
no damn good?

I felt a tap on my right shoulder. I was feeling so happy and self-absorbed
that I thought, without wonder, that it must be Nathan or God. It was a woman
in a pale pink pantsuit, carrying one small grocery bag and a white wicker purse.
She looked to be in her sixties. She said, "Please, may I join you? There's
nowhere to sit."

What could I do? I nodded as she took the chair beside me. She ordered a
screwdriver and some escargots in mushroom caps. She said, "I like a long lunch
with my friends."

I could see right away there was something *good* about her, something moth-
erly and kind. A pair of bifocals lay on her chest, hung from a golden chain, and
she'd put a blue rinse in her white waved hair. I thought of my own mother once
saying that sometimes all she really wanted was a place to lay her head but why
was it so hard to put it down there in the first place? This was after my father
had left her for a younger woman.

I was glad enough for the company of a stranger. As opposed to family and
friends, strangers will believe anything you tell them and they are less likely to
ask you what's wrong right when you thought you were doing just fine. They
will not tell you that you look tired on a day when you thought you felt terrific.
A stranger will tell you any story as if it were true. Often I have envied total
strangers on the street: just the inscrutable look of them makes it obvious that
their lives are better than mine, more normal, more simple, and perfect, yes,
perfect...perfect strangers.

"Hello," the woman said, "my name is Sheila."

I, rendered helpless in the face of coincidence, said, "Hello." It was the kind
of thing that if you put it in a story, nobody would believe it. I recovered myself
quickly enough because, after all, what possible harm could there be in exchanging
pleasantries on a pleasant afternoon with a kind woman who happened to be,
through no fault of her own, named Sheila?

It made little difference that I'm no good at small talk because this third
Sheila (or was she, chronologically speaking, because of her age rather than her
advent, the *first* Sheila?) proved to be exceedingly talkative. In the course of the

conversation, I had to tell her very little about myself, virtually nothing in fact, except to say once, when her momentum was interrupted by the arrival of dessert (chocolate almond cheesecake) and her story was stalled, that I was a writer, single, no children, said to be successful.

She told me with detailed delight about a recent trip to the mountains she'd made with her younger sister, Serena, who had the glaucoma, and how you see things differently, more clearly, more brilliantly, bright, when you have to describe and explain them to somebody else, the blind or a child.

She confided that one of the hardest things about getting older was the feeling that your body was turning on you, falling to pieces one thing at a time, and also the hair, which got thinner and thinner and she never ever wanted to become one of those sad old ladies that you can see through to their pathetic pink scalp. In high school, she said, she had been much envied for her hair which was long and lustrous, a deep burnished red, and when she marched in the school parade twirling her silver baton, her hair swung and bounced, beautiful in the sun.

She talked about her children, three of them, two boys and a girl, who were all grown-up now and living in other cities. She understood that but still, she missed them.

Mostly she talked about her husband, Victor, who had died tragically in a car crash in a snowstorm in December 1963, four days after they'd bought their first home, a brick bungalow on Addison Street downtown. She still lived in that house and every day she thought about her Victor, wondered if he'd have liked the new wallpaper in the bedroom, the beige shag carpet in the front room, the placemats, the blue towels, the new tuna casserole recipe, the microwave.

No, she'd never remarried. Things were different in those days: a new husband had never occurred to her. With her Victor gone, she just figured she'd had all she was ever going to get of or from love, for better or worse. She was satisfied, she said. She'd lived a lovely life, she said. For some things, yes, she agreed, yes, it was too late now. It was too late now to turn back. It was too late now to turn her back on what she had created: three children, the house, those long-felt heart-held memories of her Victor who, like all the young dead, had never aged, never betrayed her, never ever broke her heart again. Why would she want to change anything after all?

Why indeed? Why did I find all this so hard to believe: me with my constant chronic longing, my searching, my secret sadness at those moments when I

should have been happy, me with this an[...] or my head? "Why create trouble where t[...] asked myself now.

"Now I have this pain," she said unex[...] said, pressing the palm of her hand to her [...] scarf dramatically patterned with bright la[...]

My own hand twitched with wanting [...] was afraid there would be nothing there...

...no woman

...no breast

...no scarf

...no tigers

...just air

...the palpable eloquent air pushing dow[...] which were gathering above us.

The patio was emptying quickly under [...] women were scooping up their purses and pa[...] to just disappear.

I walked slowly back to my car in the unde[...]

I was tired suddenly and rested my head fo[...] round the steering wheel. I thought of a morni[...] Oldsmobile had pulled up suddenly in front [...] breakfast table in my nightie, hovering over m[...] driver, a stranger, a bearded young man in a pl[...] minutes with his head like this on the wheel. Th[...] me alone again, alone again to speculate in the d[...]

I hesitated as I left the parkade, not sure whi[...] route home I wanted to take. A man in a baseb[...] me leaned so hard on his horn that my eyes fi[...] insulted tears.

I turned left into the rush hour traffic and dro[...]

Sometimes on my way home from The Re[...] imagine a car (red with black interior, air scoop, [...] red light at 100 mph, rocketing through the inters[...] driver's side so that I am flung up and over, flyin[...]

...7

Point of View Revisited

THE MAKING AND BREAKING

OF THE FICTIONAL SPELL

Point of view was introduced in Chapter 6 in its relation to characterization in fiction. I am returning to it because of how often failures to understand point of view are at the root of a writer's inability to engage the reader and hold the reader through to the story's end. As an editor mentoring writers at various levels of proficiency, I probably spend more time working with point-of-view faults than with any other problem.

Most fictional stories are told from the point of view of one of the characters in the story. Consider the following two examples. They are similar fictional paragraphs differentiated only by point of view.

I looked across the stream. The evening sun had turned the water into an uneven mirror, reflecting in gold a broken image of the trees and brush on the far side. A mule deer had crept out to drink and, because the wind was in my face, I was free to watch without its sensing me.

*

He looked across the stream. The evening sun had turned the water into an uneven mirror, reflecting in gold the broken image of the trees and brush on the far side. A mule deer had crept out to drink, and because the wind was in his face, he was free to watch without its sensing him.

The point of writing those two paragraphs, so close to identical, is to illustrate how close first- and third-person points of view can be. The first paragraph (containing the first-person pronoun *I*) is first-person point of view. The second paragraph (in which the *I* is replaced by *he*) is third-person point of view.

The greatest similarity between the two ways of telling a story is that, in both, the action is perceived from the point of view of a single character. In both points of view (POVs), writer and reader have access to the same things: some or all of the thoughts of one character; some or all of what that character sees. Writer and reader are also denied access to the same things: inner thoughts of other characters; the action that the point-of-view character is not present to observe.

The difference between first- and third-person point of view is the position of the writer in relation to the POV character. In first person, the writer (therefore, the reader) is squarely in the mind of the POV character. In third person, the reader is in or out of the character's mind, or somewhere nearby. Third-person POV storytelling varies on that basis: that is, how far outside the POV character the writer sets up shop, and how much access is given to the POV character's thoughts.

In third-person fiction, there can be a great deal of access, as much as in first person. But it is also possible to write third-person fiction that almost locks the reader out of the POV character's mind. The writer and readers travel with the character, see what he or she sees, but they are not allowed into the mind and therefore must deduce from dialogue and other clues what those thoughts might be.

The difference between third-person narrations often originates in the character portrayed. One of the liberating innovations of fiction in the twentieth century was to deviate from the hyperverbal narrator, and to explore types of central characters who were perhaps great observers without being long on talk or thought. Here I think of Cormac McCarthy's characters in *All the Pretty Horses* and *The Crossing*. The characters are brief in speech and introspection, but they are eloquent in observation.

Nor should first-person fiction be thought of as one lumpen thing. "Stream of consciousness" is one of its varieties, a kind of unchecked outpouring of the workings of the mind. Probably the best-known example is the Molly Bloom soliloquy at the end of James Joyce's *Ulysses*, where Molly lies abed and thinks her wild, loquacious thoughts.

There is a type of story I will call a *reminiscent* short story that usually has two points of view representing the same human being. The story is reminiscent because it is framed as a reminiscence. It usually starts out with the character as an adult about to remember, or forced to remember, an incident from childhood. When the narration arrives in the distant past, and the story of what happened to the child begins, the narration (first- or third-person) almost always changes (and should change) into the point of view of the child. Here's an example of such a beginning, starting in the adult voice:

> *Often when it was cold at night, and ice formed on the windows, John would see the crystals exactly as they had been on the window of his first school, the window closest to his desk. Mrs. McMillan would stand at the front, yard stick in hand, and slap it into her palm, as if each fact were subdued, made flat and tame, by that action.*

As the story of the child takes over, a sudden or gradual shift into the child's POV occurs. It becomes the child's point of view, told as if it were happening now.

> *He liked the window, because it was like outside, where snow and ice made everything smooth and humpy, and where, if there was a hill underneath, you could slide. But he had to be careful too when he watched the window because teacher knew he liked it. On a bad day, to look at the window was enough reason to get the strap.*

This shift should in some subtle way change the writing, as the thoughts and actions portrayed are a child's rather than an adult's. The syntax should shift down a gear, and the vocabulary should simplify, so that the telling of the story isn't full of words and thoughts the child could not reasonably have, given his experience. This is not the same as writing entirely in a child's voice, unless the story is told in first-person POV. In third person, it's more of a suggestion of the child voice, rather than an attempt to exactly replicate it.

Usually, the reminiscent story shifts back to the adult voice at the end.

> *Marilyn, John's wife, called up from downstairs, and the illusion was suddenly shattered. The icy landscape on the window was suddenly not strong enough to hold him in that other world …*

Another variation is to shift back to the adult voice and present-time horizon within the story at major transition points.

✦ ✦ ✦ Maintaining the Point of View and Other Ways of Sustaining the Spell

A long-standing tradition in first- and third-person fiction is to stick with one point of view throughout. No less a writer than the British author Graham Greene laid it down as a kind of eleventh commandment. Greene was a realist writer of great narrative power, and he probably valued the spell that fiction casts over readers. The ideal condition of readers, as far as many authors are concerned, is to have them not be conscious of reading at all. I would like all my readers to be watching and listening more than consciously reading; to be simply inside the scenes, viewing them, experiencing them.

Because of its value, I have thought a lot about what casts this spell and what breaks it. I have concluded that a unity and consistency in the point of view is the most important way of casting the spell and maintaining it. When the point of view is established, readers place themselves with the point-of-view character and begin to live in the scenes with that character. If the character walks into a room, readers even see that room from the perspective of the door.

Of course, I am talking about good fiction. In bad fiction, readers are usually lost and getting more frustrated and bored by the minute.

Watching the story through the point-of-view character is like watching TV from your favourite chair. If you'll buy that comparison, the effect of suddenly switching readers from one person's point of view to another is like wrenching the viewer from the favourite chair and throwing that person across the room into another. Over such a disruptive shift, the story won't necessarily die, but the spell the readers have been under will necessarily break. When broken, it must be recast before the witnessing of the story can begin again. If readers liked being within the spell a certain way, they may resist viewing the story through another character, in which case you may have lost them for good.

Other types of shifting will also break the spell: sudden scene changes and time changes, for example. Some breaks are natural and intended; others are unnatural and accidental. All stories need transitions. We wrap up a scene; we move to another scene. We move from one time horizon to another. Chances are, in these moments of transition, readers remember they are readers and the spell is momentarily broken. But that's okay because you're going to begin it again somewhere else or sometime else, usually in the familiar voice that preceded the change. But to break the spell unintentionally in the midst of a scene is another matter. The effect is usually a bad one for readers, and I generally recommend that a writer not do it, unless there is some powerfully compelling reason. If not, it is better to maintain readers in a watching, engaged, feeling, and participating state as much of the time as possible.

Having said that, there are good reasons and ways of changing point of view in a story or a novel. I have done it and enjoy doing it. But my method of changing point of view within a story is to finish a scene or a chapter before the shift, and to denote the shift in some obvious way. In a story called "Round and Smooth," I alternated the point of view between a husband and wife at their two places of work, and though it sounds cute in hindsight, I called them Jack and Gill and denoted each new section with one or the other of those names in bold. In the big scene at the end (under the heading **Jack and Gill**), I favoured neither of them. I created a dual third-person point of view (as opposed to the omniscient, which we will get to momentarily). Instead of oscillating the point of view between them scene by scene, I did so paragraph by paragraph until the end. I chose to end that way because I wanted to emphasize what a couple they were, so much so that they could democratically share a scene and not lose the reader.

Another method of moving point of view between characters in a story is to use devices: letters or other documents (diary, manuscript fragments, story within a story, newspaper clippings). Many stories are made up entirely of an exchange of letters. In 2001, Richard B. Wright won both the Giller Prize and the Governor General's Award for Fiction for *Clara Callan*, a novel consisting of an exchange of letters, a type of novel called an *epistolary* novel.

In a story of my own called "Working Without a Laugh Track" (the title story of a 1990 collection), there are two important characters; a comedian and his sister, who live on opposite sides of the continent. Everything in the story is from one of her letters to him or from one of his stand-up comedy routines. The motivation for writing the story that way was that the sister uses her letters to her brother to emotionally clean house. She is candid about her family—and very funny. But only the discourse is funny; she's actually very depressed. We find out from her letters that her brother never visits and never writes or phones back. He is incommunicado, and she doesn't even know if the letters reach him. What we find out from his comedy routines is that he lives off his sister's letters. All her jokes and sayings are found in his comedy routines. We also find out that he is a failing comedian, heading sharply downward.

✦ ✦ ✦ Omniscient Point of View: The Godlike POV

The omniscient point of view is different from any of the methods of narration mentioned thus far. It is narrated, in a sense, from above. Some call it the Voice-of-God point of view because it can see all and can go anywhere. The narrative can dip into the thoughts of any of the characters, can describe scenes and events that have one, some, or all of the characters of the story in them— or none. Why not, if it helps fill out the historical tableaux, go back in time before the characters were born? Or ahead to a time after their deaths?

It no doubt sounds tantalizing. The lack of constraints. The many apparent advantages. But it might be a good idea before you embark on anything ambitious in the omniscient voice that you try several experiments. Many metaphors could describe this form of narration; for example, participating in a road race without a track. You can drive anywhere you like, at any speed you like, to any destination—which would be great, except you might never see the other drivers you are trying to outdrive, and you would never know when you had begun, or when the race was over, or who had won.

You will probably find, as I have, that it is hard to involve the reader in the omniscient voice, to maintain the reader's interest and not confuse when you don't have a consistent character to perceive action through. It is harder to cast the spell in other words, and you have many more ways to break it. It's also how *War and Peace* is written, lest I seem to be suggesting it is a lesser type of fictional narration. Often choice of point of view boils down to style. The omniscient POV was more popular in the nineteenth century. First and third person were more popular in the twentieth. Toward the end of the twentieth century, there was a round of second-person short stories.

> When you get to the store, Mr. Pickles, the storekeeper is pleased to see you. He acts exactly as if you haven't been there for a week, rather than the twenty minutes it has been. You wonder if you are that transparent, that unmemorable to Mr. Pickles, and the day in some unrecoverable way is ruined.

Second-person point of view was an experiment that most writers had a go at in this period. Such experiments are the focus of the next section.

✦ ✦ ✦ Experiments in Point of View

I am conscious of a kind of disciplinarian quality to this chapter, and I would like to lighten up. Playing with point of view in fiction is also where a lot of the fun can be. Once you have the conventions in hand, you can play with and confound readers' expectations in pleasurable ways (pleasurable for them and for you). One of my favourite examples is the story you read to prepare for this chapter, Diane Schoemperlen's "Stranger Than Fiction."

The convention of the third-person point of view is that the narrator is a neutral voice, speaking the story of one of the characters. Sometimes that point of view is called third-person-limited to emphasize that it is limited to one character and does not speak the thoughts or see through the eyes of any other. In "Stranger Than Fiction," the narrator is anything but a wallflower. She is an individual with a story of her own. The third-person story she is telling/writing about her fictional character named Sheila is often secondary to the author's story. If you remember the end of the story, you are with the author/narrator in her life, which suggests that the story is about her, and the way the making of fiction influences her life. It is not finally about Sheila, the fictional character. The ending relates back to the beginning: the mini-essay that introduced the ideas of coincidence and the strange relationship between truth and fiction that the story has explored.

What you would be well advised *not* to assume about this story is that the narrator/author is Diane Schoemperlen. The *I* of the story, though proclaiming herself the author of the story, the creator of the fictional Sheila and the fictional Carlos, is a fiction herself, which adds to the humour, the row-of-mirrors effect that the story produces and plays with.

The opinionated author starts out by telling readers about the fictional Sheila, about her fictional life, her marriage to Roger, her desire to be a country-and-western singer. She tells of Sheila's meeting with Carlos (a country-and-western singer) in a record store, where by coincidence they are both looking for the same Patsy Cline album.

The author tells her story in a confiding way, the way you might tell a friend about some antic neighbour over coffee. The effect is that our disbelief is suspended. We start believing in Sheila in the way that we ordinarily believe in well-drawn, convincingly presented fictional characters, even though the author keeps reminding us that Sheila is only an invention.

So then I made Sheila unhappy in her heart of hearts: because what's a good story without a little angst?

Then comes another surprise move. The author, whom we are trained as readers to expect will be anonymous, starts telling about herself. As if it were a normal coincidence, she tells us that she too has met a fellow (just like Sheila has), and compares the unfolding of her romance to Sheila's romance with Carlos.

Many times in the story, the author steps out of her fictional work and her personal story to reflect aloud on the echoes and responses between her life and observations and her current fiction project.

I am accustomed by now to the habit fiction has of assuming the guise of reality.

Sentences like "stranger things have happened" appear frequently in the story as echoes of the opening frame which promised the story would be a reflection on what is stranger than fiction in life and how fiction relates to life if you're a writer.

When Diane Schoemperlen gets the story to where readers are comfortable with its dual point of view—its two stories advancing side by side, the expansive, chatty, confiding narrator, and so on—she springs another surprise. The author/narrator starts thinking of a girl she went to school with, another Sheila, who no one was nice to, who had a baby without knowing she was pregnant; the urban myth come true. Suddenly because of this memory, the fictional Sheila starts to exhibit traits of the plain Sheila from the author's school days. The fictional one loses her energy; she starts eating way too much. The author has to put her foot down and demand that she stop it.

At the story's end, the author is driving home, turning every person she sees, everything in her path, into fiction. She does so whether she wants to or not.

So far, I have not mentioned that Diane Schoemperlen's story is funny. Partly it is funny because that is one of her great gifts as a writer, which she brings to most of her fiction. The story is also funny because the author has an amusing address, the way the rare person can tell a story and make it funny by the way it is told. She spins off into tangents at unexpected moments and at unexpected angles.

The story is also funny because of the play with point of view. Because of what the reader expects of a piece of fiction, the effect of the garrulous author/narrator is at once funny. Accustomed to authors performing their tricks of story-telling behind the scenes, the reader laughs to see this author/narrator step in front of the curtain and tell us what she's doing and about to do; she confides in us her problems of controlling and confining the act of authorship to the printed page.

If you are interested in how fiction is categorized, this story would be regarded in some circles as postmodern: it challenges the rules and assumptions of the modern short story, which sought to achieve high realism, a convincing facsimile of the real world. Postmodernism in literature challenges assumptions such as that fiction is or wants to be a representation of the real, and that the narration in a story must be honest, faithful, and largely invisible.

The postmodern stance asks compelling questions.

Why would you ever believe a work that you know is fiction? Why does a narrator have to be faithful and earnest? Why can't he or she be unreliable instead? Why can't the writer of the story surface and discuss what's going on in the attempt to make the character seem this way or that? Why not use fiction as a place to examine what fiction is; what words are for?

The amusing point about terms like modern and postmodern is how ironic they become as the decades pass. Modernism, as a literary movement, is most associated with the first decades of the twentieth century. Postmodernism is many decades old as well, an elderly ingenue.

Some postmodern questions and experiments were not new even when post-modernism was new as a theory of literature. We sometimes think that fiction writing began with an emphasis on tightness, control, and adherence to ortho-doxy, and that it loosened up and became more self-satirizing (more interesting) with time. But, in fiction, not so. *Don Quixote*, written by Miguel de Cervantes in 1605, one of the world's oldest novels, was a satire of the age of chivalry. It lampooned the terminology and the type of romantic story that had grown out of that age. The narration conveys much of the satire, such as when the narrator describes Don Quixote as the "knight of the rueful countenance."

It's a distant time-travel from *Don Quixote* to "Stranger Than Fiction," but there is a relationship between them, a similar playfulness and tendency to sati-rize what we normally allow the narrator of a fiction to know and do. It probably was not Diane Schoemperlen's purpose in writing "Stranger Than Fiction," but she has provided aspiring writers with an enjoyable example of how to turn the conventions of point of view and narration on their ear, for humorous effect.

✦ ✦ ✦ Your Process

- Take one of the short-story ideas you developed in an earlier exercise and write the first page using a first-person point of view.

- Convert this first page into third-person-limited point of view.

- Convert the page again so that it is told by an omniscient narrator (one who can see all the events and knows all the character's thoughts but is not a character in the story).

- Go back to the third-person point-of-view version, and transform the narrator from a neutral voice telling the story through one of the characters into a character who has his or her own feelings about the proceedings, who besides narrating the story character's tale has his or her own story to tell.

- If your author/narrator is not already an unreliable narrator, transform him or her into one. Have the narrator lie about the character or about himself or herself—and then reveal the lie.

- Think about, or write a mini-essay about, the differences in the relationship between the writer and the reader in each of the five versions of this opening page.

Story Beginnings

HOOKING, GUIDING,

AND INFORMING

How should a short story begin? Some blunt and all-encompassing things have been said on this subject. Given the almost limitless capacity of writers to begin stories in new and effective ways, nothing so final will be said here.

Edgar Allan Poe's fiction definition, quoted in Chapter 3, implies that if you blow your first line or paragraph, all is lost. It is true that no story can afford to begin ineffectively, but the insistence of some that the story always begin with *impact!* has led to excess.

> *Blood suddenly oozed under the door.*
> *She looked up and the elevator streaked down the shaft toward her.*

It may not be wrong to try hard to rivet attention at the outset, but a study of how skilful writers begin short stories yields the truth that nothing needs to explode, no one needs to die, in sentence one.

Though the emphasis of this chapter will be on the short story, much of what I write here applies equally to the novel. The need to hook a reader off the top may seem to be a short-story thing rather than a novel thing, but let's not be too quick to assume. If people buy a magazine with a short story in it, they'll probably read the story because they own the magazine, whether it has a whiz-bang beginning or not. If as various studies suggest, readers go into a bookstore most often not knowing what they want to buy, then maybe the first page of a novel needs a hook as much or more than a short story does. Maybe it needs that hook as much as it needs a fancy cover and a provocative title.

For purposes of comparison, I've reread the first lines of many favourite novels, and I see no important differences compared to short-story beginnings. The effort to hook readers, the planting of an important question, the introduction of characters, are all present.

Let's consider what a reader is doing as a short story or novel begins. The idea that a story must begin with a bang is based on the idea that a reader (or editor, perhaps more to the point) is approaching a story or novel with enormous scepticism and dozens of other pressing things to do. That much may be true, but this big-bang opening theory also implies that readers aren't subtle or wide-ranging in terms of what will grab their attention. A short-story beginning should be interesting, but who can define what that means? Startling, amusing, intriguing, stylish—soothing even? The beginning must pose a question of sufficient interest that readers read on in search of an answer. Many writers do begin a story with the assumption of dedicated readers who won't stop dead just because the first sentence hasn't made them sweat with anxiety. Others begin with the assumption that readers take a minute or so to get their interest engaged. Those writers don't pack the first sentences with facts readers must grasp to understand the story.

My concern with fictional beginnings is that readers, at the outset of a story, are trying to orientate themselves. It is almost as though you had transported them somewhere blindfolded, and now you have removed the blindfold. Just because they can see doesn't mean they know where they are. Most readers don't have patience with writers who begin a story by being mysterious. Why would a writer try to confuse and mystify the reader in the opening paragraphs? I have never understood this approach and would rather make it as easy for my readers as possible. In addition to getting their interest, I'm also trying to let them know the basics of where they are, when, with whom, and so on.

If you recall, "The Dog in the Van" has that kind of beginning.

It was an old blue Chevy van with newly painted white bumpers.

After describing the van, where it is and for how long every day, the first sentence of the second paragraph introduces the dog who sits locked in the van behind the closed windows. The Crossleys, Jan and Dick, see the dog in the van every day on the way in and out of work at the university. From the beginning, they are arguing about what the dog in the van means.

For some reason when the author writes "It was an old blue Chevy van," the sentence has a provocative effect. Readers ask, "Where? By the river? In an accident? In front of your house?" There is the implication that something is amiss with the van, suspicious about it, and you read on to find out what. What's suspicious is a dog locked in it for hours with the windows rolled up; and that situation engages our feelings about pets and their treatment by undeserving masters. It sometimes seems that people are more concerned with the treatment of animals, their well-being, than with the well-being of adult humans. Pets, like children, are innocents, and we think they should be treated well. At that point, the hook is in. The readers—like Jan Crossley—want an explanation.

In a list of types of story beginnings, this one might be called *a description of setting.* The story goes a few other places, but the van where the dog is imprisoned is the key location in the story, and it is described. Unless a description of setting includes some portent, some question, it will not work as a beginning. But Greg Hollingshead gives us those portents and seeds those questions, and the story beginning is strong.

"Half-Past Eight" begins with Tessie painstakingly putting on lipstick, in preparation for the Calgary Stampede Parade. In "Visitation," Almeida is going to the door to answer the doorbell, dreaming that her visitor has come to tell her that it was a mistake, that her daughter is alive and well. You might call both these beginnings *a major character in action.*

Certainly, if we compare the three stories, in terms of putting a narrative hook in the reader, "Visitation" takes the ribbon. The questions seeded by that story's opening are the most provocative. What has happened to the daughter? Who is at the door? In "The Dog in the Van," the question is almost as provocative (who has imprisoned this poor dog?), but the dog is after all still a dog.

The hook in "Half-Past Eight" is more subtle, but still there. The process for readers is that they are figuring out the character from the clues given. It is a woman, a woman putting on lipstick, a woman putting on a cheap, perfumed kind of lipstick. We recognize the truth of what we're being shown, and there is a question too. Where is this older woman, the one with the perfumed lipstick, preparing to go?

The beginning doesn't have to launch you into the story with the force of a catapult, but it does have to move you there through planting a question that seeks an answer.

The story beginning usually gets the characters onto the story stage. In the Hollingshead, Alford, and Wyatt stories, the major characters are present before the first two paragraphs are complete. Dick and Jan Crossley, and the dog in the van, arrive right off the top. Only Larry, the dog's owner, remains for us to meet later. Bringing Larry in later is part of the story's suspense.

Tessie is alone in her room at the beginning of "Half-Past Eight." We don't meet Flora on page one, though she is mentioned as Tessie's partner in crime on page two. But Flora is not the protagonist of the story. Tessie is. It is fitting that Tessie is onstage first and alone.

Almeida and Martha are met at the beginning of "Visitation." Joe is an important character but not in a way that demands his presence; the story is about Almeida and how her cousin Martha tortures her unwittingly. Both characters are in the scene by paragraph two.

Lest I give the impression that story beginnings are never, or should never be, flashy, let's consider one that is. Here's the beginning of "An Occurrence at Owl Bridge," a nineteenth-century story by American author Ambrose Bierce:

A man stood upon a railroad bridge in northern Alabama, looking down into the swift water twenty feet below. The man's hands were behind his back, his wrists bound with a cord. A rope closely encircled his neck.

This opening is a more aggressive demand for our attention. We can hardly help but wonder what will happen next. Intriguing too is the way this beginning makes us want to know why it's happening in the first place. That is, Bierce seeds a question about what precedes the moment that is as powerful as the question about what follows it.

The beginning should fit the story, but that is not always remembered in the quest for a dramatic opening. Only a story about a hanging should begin with a hanging.

The way the writer gets the attention of readers does not always have to do with character and plot. Some stories use an intriguing sentence or phrase to begin the engagement of the readers, and that's what we find in "Stranger Than Fiction."

"Any number of people will tell you that truth is stranger than fiction," Schoemperlen begins. This opening intrigues us because we know what we are about to read is a short story. Instead of beginning a story, the narrator tells us a few tall-tale examples of truth's strangeness. The opening section is a tour de force splash of intriguing, comically exaggerated examples and we are hooked not so much by our desire to answer a plot question but because we enjoyed the humour and the experience. We hope there's more where that came from.

Another nineteenth-century American, the prolific O. Henry, was famous for his "twist endings." But as H.E. Bates says in *The Modern Short Story*, O. Henry should be acknowledged too for what he did with beginnings. O. Henry stripped his story openings of any lengthy preamble and got to the meat of things. He almost invariably began with some amusing, intriguing statement.

So I went to the doctor. "How long has it been since you took alcohol into your system?" he asked.

A story with a moral appended is like the bill of a mosquito. It bores you, and then injects a stinging drop to irritate your conscience. Therefore let us have the moral first and be done with it.

✦ ✦ ✦ Story Beginnings

Stories begin with:
* a description of place, an important story setting
* a main character in action
* an event that rivets attention
* an amusing or intriguing statement

Beginnings help to:
* orientate readers
* introduce or imply the presence of key characters
* put questions in the minds of readers
* lure readers into continuing to read

✦ ✦ ✦ Exposition

A dictionary definition of exposition is *setting forth; description; explanation; commentary*. Its meaning in fiction is *that which the reader needs to know to understand the story*. In the preceding section, I gave a testimonial on behalf of helping readers find their way at the opening of a story. Now, I caution about what can happen when the writer tries too hard at the outset to do so. That is, look out for the tendency to lump the entire exposition into the opening page. All too often the result is an unintentional moment of comedy.

In the theatre, an old convention was "the serving scene." A play would open with two servants tidying up downstairs:

Maid: I guess the master will be returning soon.
Butler: Yes, from the Congo, where he has been prospecting for gold for three long years now, while m'lady waited and pined.
Maid: Yes, waited and pined, until she could stand it no longer and allowed herself to be seduced by that cad, Carlton Smythe.
Butler: Frankly, I worry that when the master gets back, with his elephant gun and his bad temper, and discovers that Smythe has been …

This convention got the exposition out of the way without wasting time and ingenuity. But if your fictional exposition starts to sound like this scene, it's not a good thing.

What is wrong with bunching exposition at the start of a story is that the story then does not originate in the characters but rather in the author, who is trying to squeeze it in. The exposition lacks a natural place, and worse, lacks motivation. If there is no good reason for a character to think a thing, and the author forces the character to think it, the thing will stick out awkwardly. It will never seem at home in the story because it isn't.

> Smith walked to the sink and looked for a spatula in the pile of unwashed dishes. Holding more and more dishes in his arms, he thought of the six years he had spent training lions for the circus. Finally, there it was, at the very bottom—the spatula.

If you are writing first-person or third-person narration, exposition is a simple matter of putting the facts you need into the story when there is a reason for the character to be thinking or talking about them. If exposition is motivated, it will be smooth and seamless. If not, it will be a bump in the story that jolts you at every reading.

Writers often assume readers need more information than they do, or assume they need it before they do. Pare down to the minimum where exposition is concerned, unless the information is fascinating and your character has good reason to present it in detail and at length. You don't want to slot in a fact two sentences before it is needed. That always looks contrived. But there's also not much sense in putting it at the beginning if it is needed near the end. I am an ordinary reader of fiction, and I am forgetful. If a fact comes too early, I will forget it if the reason for its inclusion doesn't show up soon.

The ideal for exposition is invisibility: to make readers learn the needed facts without their knowing that you forced those facts upon them.

Consider how Edna Alford establishes the fact that Tessie and Flora like a drink. The first mention of liquor is when Tessie is thinking about how difficult it has been for her to save twenty dollars from her Veterans Affairs Pension. To save money for today, "She hadn't bought a drop of liquor in all that time."

The statement is motivated because it relates to the topic Tessie is thinking about: the way she saved money for parade day. It is thrown away at the end of the paragraph, but it also hits hard because of that placement. The reader thinks: "Ah, so she drinks." The reader knows it is important to her because not drinking is cited as a sacrifice. If she seldom drank, not drinking wouldn't save her much money.

The second time drinking comes up is when Tessie is thinking about what makes her friendship with Flora work. She thinks it is because they are alike: game, fun, willing to take a chance. It's not the drinking, she says, which is the opinion of the other old biddies. In the first two references to drinking, she stresses that liquor is something she can do without, something that isn't as important to her friendship with Flora as people say. She is denying that liquor is important, and who but a fairly serious drinker ever does that?

Exposition, to be effective yet unobtrusive, needs to be motivated from within the story. It is never enough that the author feels the information needs to be present. A reason must exist within the story for the fact to come out. Ask yourself what the reader really needs to know. It is often less than you think. Exposition doesn't need to be, nor should it ever be, packed into the opening of the story.

The best openings are those without extensive preamble, particularly if the stories are realist. Another rule of story openings is to start as deeply into the action as you possibly can, so the story is up and running and propelling readers forward before they have time to question their reasons for reading on.

Still, when I think of what a story opening should or shouldn't be, I always remember the opening line of Anton Chekhov's story "The Darling":

> Olenka, the daughter of the retired collegiate assessor Plemyanikov, was sitting on the back-door steps of her house doing nothing.

✦ ✦ ✦ Your Process

Return to the story beginnings you have already written and rewrite them as follows, or begin a new story or two.

- Write a story beginning that puts your main character in action in a way that provokes at least one important story question for readers.

- Try a story beginning that begins not with a human performing an action but with an important object or animal in the story. ("The Dog in the Van" could be the model here.) Describe the object or animal in a way that provokes important questions for the reader. (Remember the idea of the catalyst. Maybe the object or animal is your story's catalyst, provoking the story into being.)

- Begin a story with an intriguing or amusing statement. Then spring off that statement into a beginning that establishes where we are, whom we are with, and provokes a question that will make the reader read on.

- Begin a story with a mini-essay. Describe what your character thinks about the subject at the heart of the story. Write the mini-essay in the voice of a story character or in the voice of a personified narrator (as in "Stranger Than Fiction"). Then make a transition to the story.

- Go as far into a first draft as you can in one sitting with the most promising of these beginnings. (If it's not far, don't worry.) Try one of the other beginnings to see if it will take you farther. Go as far as inspiration and time permit before you stop.

...9
High Point, Ending, Title

As the title suggests, I believe that the high point of a story, its ending, and its title are related in an important fashion, and should always be considered together, both when writing and when revising. All three should be created and revised in relation to one another.

✦ ✦ ✦ High Point and Ending

In Chapters 4 and 5, the dramatic arc that leads to an action climax was discussed. I used "The Dog in the Van" as an example of a story that leads to a big action climax: when the dog is throwing itself around the van in the storm and Dick Crossley tries to do something about it, and fails. This event is the highest point of action, and it changes Dick. When he next talks to his wife, he is different: more direct, more demanding. What this difference will cause exists beyond the story. "The Dog in the Van" is an example of a story that employs what I call "the big scene," an extended, active, and explosive moment. Often, it is delineated more than other scenes.

To show how differently the big scene can be presented, think back to the end of Edna Alford's "Half-Past Eight." A good question is whether the big scene is when Flora feels Tessie's leg at the lounge and shatters the fun of the evening, causing Tessie to demand to go home, or if it is when Flora is singing her dirty song into the silence of the nursing home. It could be argued either way. It could even be said that the story has two climaxes, each one doing something different. The first moment (Flora feeling Tessie's leg) is the action climax, the climax of their drunkenness, the peak of the chaos that has been gathering in the lounge as they become more inebriated, less in control. The question has been where this chaos was leading, and now it is answered.

The scene that follows deals with the deeper meaning of the story, with its meaning for Tessie, who is the story's protagonist. The rule of thumb is that a story's climax, pivot, major change, or new understanding must affect the protagonist. Its impact on the protagonist is the story. The day of the Stampede Parade changes for Tessie when Flora feels up her leg, but the lasting effect, the meaning of the change, is revealed back at the nursing home. Flora singing the dirty song and weaving down the hall, smashing into the walls, is her challenge against old age. She's not like the rest of them, those pitiful ones who can stay up only until half-past seven. Flora can stay up until half-past eight. One hour. The difference between Flora and Tessie and everyone else, the difference they are counting on for their self-respect, is that slender hour.

Often in short fiction, the high point (call it climax or culmination or any of its other names) produces the beginning of an emotional effect that has its full effect beyond that moment. The function of the part of the story after the climax is often to provide a place where this emotional impact can land. Dick Crossley is transformed by the storm. Something happens to him. We find out what has happened during his conversation with his wife when he states his demands. But, at the end, there is the dog, the catalyst, waiting for him with its doggy grin, representing all that he cannot control or change. That is the emotional ending of the story.

In "Half-Past Eight," the moment in the bar when Flora feels Tessie's leg and Tessie becomes angry climaxes the parade day, breaks it off, forces it to end. But Edna Alford does not stop there: she sends readers back with Flora and Tessie to witness the emotional conclusion of the day. Flora is still battling in her loud, abrasive, almost violent way, battling against old age and the expectations people have that the old will accept a small life. Tessie will get over her annoyance that her friend has made a pass at her. Probably it has happened before. She still admires Flora, still counts on Flora to keep her from lapsing into a smaller old age. But readers are also given an image that is sad and hard to shake. The image is of Tessie, her pale face projecting out of the dark like a white mask; her makeup, which she spent so much time preparing, now a disaster of running mascara. The journey for readers began with the preparation of Tessie's makeup (beginning, preparation, advent, excitement), and now it comes full circle to the melting down of that makeup into something bedraggled and sad (ending, loss, disappointment, pathos).

In earlier chapters, "Visitation" has been described as a story that leads not to an action climax, not to a big scene or a noticeable high point. It leads instead to an emotional pivot, a new understanding, what Joyce called an epiphany. Whereas Almeida has dreamed of a dramatic ending for this visit from Martha, the revelation is that she is too civilized to provide it. She will not kick her interfering cousin down the steps. She will not even rebuke her. She will thank her for coming, for caring, even though Martha has made the day worse. But something did happen, and the ending of the story, the part beyond that epiphany, is again the place where the emotional changes land. After Martha, something is changed in this house of mourning. Almeida is pushing herself to look forward, to the fixing of swings and the cooking of soufflés. She will act as if the future matters, and therefore, in time, the future will matter again.

In the traditional structure of drama, the part beyond climax is called *denouement.* It is the place in a story where loose ends are tied up. I always think of the *Perry Mason* television series of my childhood where, in the climax of the show, Perry would by some deft trickery force a revelation in the courtroom, produce a confession, catch a witness out in a fatal lie. Then all we watchers would be taken to commercial. After that final commercial, Perry and his assistant and others would be sitting around the office, and one or more of them would ask how he'd done it. Anything that wasn't obvious from the turn of events in the courtroom would be explained by Perry now, and so the viewers could go away fully satisfied. It was a classic *denouement.*

The word denouement does not describe well what is going on in the final moments of most short stories. Plot often isn't what a short story is about. If boiled down to plot, literary short stories can appear simple. Two elderly women go to the parade, get drunk, have a fight, go home. An abused dog creates conflict in a marriage; the dog cannot produce a solution, so no solution is found. A cousin unexpectedly visits a grieving mother; the cousin by her emotional ham-handedness produces pain but also, inadvertently, produces change.

What is complex in a literary short story is its examination and revelation of the emotional and psychological workings of the human mind, and that is what the ending of a literary short story is all about, not the tying up of loose ends, but the landing, the impact of the emotional and psychological story that has been told.

Instead of tying up loose ends, a short-story ending (beyond climax or epiphany) is often a place where the emotions of the story are allowed to reverberate. The story has produced an emotional effect. In the ending, those emotions echo and go deeper. So when we see Tessie from a distance in the nursing home with her mascara in streaks, her face like a mask, we grieve for her and we grieve for ourselves, for everyone who must grow old, battle against aging, and inevitably lose.

Another function of the ending beyond climax is to suggest where the lives of these people will go next. That is, the meaning of the action of the story and the climax or epiphany is signalled by a subtle suggestion of the future. At the end of "Visitation," Almeida admits that she still wants to hide, especially from the people who will say the unbearable thing: that life must go on. But she forces herself out the door. She forces herself down the street, because unless she does, she cannot make the soufflé. She cannot go forward in her life.

In "The Dog in the Van," the unwanted catalyst, the now-bandaged dog, runs up, not to Jan who wants him and loves him, but to Dick. The dog crinkles his lip and smiles at Dick. The dog that represents everything in life Dick is afraid of and can't control, especially what he cannot control in his own marriage, is standing there before him, smiling as if to say, "I'm still here. You haven't got away from me."

In "Stranger Than Fiction," the story has been about the author's ability to shape the fictional world, and the way the world when shaped in fiction starts to feed back, starts to affect the author's life. The story's ending has the author-as-character in her car, imagining various scenarios. She imagines being hit by another car in an intersection and mutilated beyond recognition. She imagines being other people on the crosswalks, strangers, innocents, their lives suddenly changed or erased by a random event. She imagines herself as the driver deliberately doing all this damage. Then she imagines they are not bodies but balloons "of all colours, full of wonder, words, and hot air, bobbing up and away, bouncing off asphalt, the rooftops, the pain, and a cloud."

As with most everything else in this unconventional narrative, it's hard to say what the ending is doing. But the types of imagining—the creating of a fiction out of the real, making a story and then playing all the parts—is like a summation of fiction writing. As a practice, it is both delightful and dark, voluntary and compulsive, sane and not so sane. The narrator cannot stop spinning scenarios. It is her fate, and as a fate, it is ambiguous. It's hard to say even if it is a happy or sad condition.

✦ ✦ ✦ Title

My beliefs about titling are simple. The word or words should have eye appeal. They should be attractive or intriguing or shocking in some way. They should have a good sound. They should have emotional power.

The words of a title should have one connotation for readers before they read the story, and then different connotations along the way and by the story's end. As the story progresses, the meaning of the title should change for readers. Maybe the meaning changes only once; maybe it changes several times. Often the meaning or flavour for readers is changed one last time, or given one more push by the writer, in the last sentence.

"Stranger Than Fiction" is a title drawn from a familiar phrase: "Truth is stranger than fiction." But the story is playful and clever, and even profound, as it delineates the strange relationship between strange life and strange fiction. It introduces us to various ways the fiction writer is influenced by strange aspects of life to create fiction from them. It becomes a funny story the more it pokes fun at the almost helpless fiction writer who takes in life and transforms it into fiction. This story particularly pokes fun at the image of the writer as maestro in control of literary effects. It presents instead a vision of a writer who is impulsive, almost helpless, in the way her biography mixes with and dictates her fiction.

The meaning of the title keeps bending and shifting and multiplying as Diane Schoemperlen presents, through her twin protagonists, more and different ways that life and fiction relate strangely.

The title "The Dog in the Van" seems almost pedestrian at first. The story contains a dog in a van. But the meaning of the dog in the van is not static. The effect of the dog keeps growing until it has thrown the lives of the people observing it and reacting to it into a blender on purée. It is an example of a class of titles that I will call *naming the story after the catalyst*.

If there is a catalyst in a short story, the author will often choose the catalyst as the key word in the title. Earlier, I mentioned a story of a family pushed into crisis by an infestation of bugs. The story I had in mind was "Bugs" by British Columbia author Nancy Holmes. Similarly, in Guy de Maupassant's classic story "The Necklace," the necklace is a catalyst that brings about a series of disasters.

In my story "Teeth," I used the protagonist's body parts (teeth) as a catalyst. Cowardly and reluctant NHL hockey player Doug Burns is summed up by the fact that he has all of his teeth and is obsessed with keeping them in mint condition. How many real-life hockey players have all their teeth? Probably not one. The story leads to a big scene, a hockey fight, which Doug as usual works to avoid. He is standing by the boards, daydreaming about an old girlfriend, and he is grabbed by the only other player in the bench-clearing brawl who doesn't have a "dance partner." This player promptly butts out Doug's front tooth with his head. All through the story, Doug has been dickering with the question of whether he should leave professional hockey. It has been largely theoretical. Suddenly, the catalyst speaks. A tooth is gone, "a hole in his head for life," and the decision is theoretical no longer. The moment the catalyst is driven from his head is the moment of epiphany.

As a title, "Teeth" has one meaning for the reader at the beginning. Whatever the reader thinks of teeth will be attached to it. It is short. It is odd. I hope it is intriguing. The first change comes when the reader knows the story is about hockey. Teeth, in hockey, are ironic. "Teeth" as the title of a hockey story produces the image of teeth knocked out, teeth broken, toothless players giving television interviews, false teeth put in after the game. When the story reveals that Doug has all his teeth and is fussy about them, the title changes again. It now defines his difference as a hockey player. He must be a cowardly player, an excellent avoider of conflict, to manage to keep a full set of teeth. At the end, the title changes meaning again. Doug loses his first tooth to the game of hockey. He is defiled by his sport. He is paying a price in teeth for the money he earns. The title defines his choice: Go or stay?

Titles often play with a word's duality of meaning or with its connotations. "Visitation" is about a visit, an unwanted one. Why not call it "Visit"? Consider the difference between a visit and a visitation. A visit is a homely little thing, something you would want. "Visitation" is defined in the Oxford dictionary as an *official visit of inspection, an unusually protracted visit or social call.* Examples are given: *a bishop's examination of the churches of the diocese, the boarding of a vessel belonging to another state to learn her character or purpose.* As the story goes along and Martha's purposes in coming become more bizarre, especially the attempt to lure Almeida to her health farm, *visit* does indeed become *visitation.* Almeida's ship of grief has been boarded. This title would belong to a class of titles called *plays on key words.*

"Half-Past Eight" is a title I would class as *a mystery.* Readers can't initially guess—not correctly at least—what it means. It is a time of day. Full stop. As readers, we don't even know whether the title refers to morning or evening, and we can't have a set of connotations without that knowledge.

But what does the title compel us to ask? What will happen at half-past eight? Something will happen that is important enough to cause it to be chosen as a title.

Now, let's look at when the answer to the mystery is revealed. The answer does not come until the end of the story. First, we discover it is when Flora and Tessie arrive back at the nursing home. It is shockingly early. When we think of what has happened, the parade, the drinking, and so on, the reader might have imagined a later hour. In most lives, it probably would have been a later hour. But that is the point. When Flora is embarked on her final, desperate, drunken, brawling disruption of the nursing home, "half-past eight" means to her the difference between the two friends, the revellers, and all the other old ladies in the home, who can only stay up until half-past seven. Flora and Tessie stay up until half-past eight!

What Edna Alford is doing here is pointing out the difference not just between Flora and Tessie and the other elderly women, but the difference between the readers and the characters in the story. There are different connotations for this time of evening, but for most readers, half-past eight viewed as a time of returning after your big event of the year is early. The title then becomes a measurement in the experience of old age. There may come a time when half-past eight defines bedtime, or a time past it, especially if we land in an institution, abiding by restrictive laws. The one-hour difference is the margin of difference and of freedom; the defining difference, slender as it is.

The title's mystery is not solved until the final moment. Whatever we thought the title meant, we were likely wrong. The meaning is resolved at the end, when all good mysteries are.

"Stranger Than Fiction" is different again. Let's call it a member of the *familiar phrase* class or maybe a different class of titles that are *puzzles* for readers to solve. Here the writer is very definitely using the connotations of a familiar phrase as a beginning. Usually, with this type of story title, the writer will by the end, stand the usual connotation of the familiar phrase on its ear. For example, if you were to title a story "The Sunday Picnic," it would immediately flower into connotations of pleasant outings, of family rituals, of summer days. An author's intention might be to have something ghastly happen at such an occasion, in which case the title would become heavily ironic.

As a final example of titling, I would like to use one of my story titles. It's probably not an instructive anecdote because I doubt that anyone would want to follow my example. I used the title as a place to put a fact I liked but couldn't find a home for anywhere inside the story. The story was set in the days leading up to the first-ever Calgary Stampede, and it culminated in a tragedy: a cowboy was killed while testing broncs for the bucking events. The man who was killed was Joe La Mar and the horse that killed him was called Red Wings. The historical fact that I couldn't place inside the story was that another cowboy named Emery Legrandeur rode Red Wings, in an untimed exhibition ride at another rodeo, well after Joe La Mar was killed. I couldn't place the fact in the story because it happened after the story, and the story was not the kind of story where foreshadowings or leaps into the future would have worked. So I made it the title: *A Year Before Emery Legrandeur Rode Red Wings to a Standstill and Avenged the Death of Joe La Mar.*

To return to this chapter's title: why then are high point, ending, and title grouped together? My purpose is to emphasize that you can't select a good title, except by accident, until you know how your story has ended and what it is about. In other words, it's a good idea to go with a working title, and then come back to the matter of titling after everything else is done.

✦ ✦ ✦ **Fiction Titles**

Here are some classes of titles for you to consider and use:

- direct reference to what the story is about
- the name of the story's catalyst
- plays on words related to the story
- mysteries
- puzzles
- plays on the connotations of a familiar phrase

───────────────────────────────────────

A danger to look out for is the title that is wonderful for something but not for this story or novel. A writer can fall in love with a title for its own sake and saddle a story or novel with it because of that fondness. As writers (which Diane Schoemperlen illustrates so nicely in "Stranger than Fiction"), we are endlessly able to rationalize what we are doing in fiction as correct. Protecting a beloved title against its inadequacy can be one of those rationalizations.

✦ ✦ ✦ Your Process

✦ Complete the first draft of the story you began after the last chapter. Try for a story length of around three thousand words. (You made several beginnings. Proceed with the one that excites you most.)

✦ Describe in a paragraph what kind of high point or turning point your story led to. Did it have an action climax in a big scene, an epiphany (quiet but important), or an event that marked or triggered a turning point in the life of the character?

✦ Come up with five titles for your story. Out of the five, try for one that is intriguing for readers even without any knowledge of the story, but whose meaning will change as the story progresses. If the title changes meaning only once, it should change near the end. Hint: the words of a title are often found somewhere in the story (e.g. "Half-Past Eight," "Stranger Than Fiction").

...*10*

Mood and Rhythm

THE MYSTERIES OF STYLE

When I embarked on this self-directed course in fiction writing, I vowed not to duck the subject of style. In my brief time as a university student, I noticed that English professors generally avoided discussions of literary style, which amazed me then. How could you talk about James Joyce's *Ulysses* or Leonard Cohen's *Beautiful Losers* or Alice Munro's works without talking about that which sets them apart from one another? But my professors could and did. Their reason may have been that these were not courses in writing, or it might have been that a writer's style is a hard thing to talk about. Or maybe it's easy enough to talk about but not so easy to make sense of. Style is fundamental to the craft of fiction so it will be talked of here.

✦ ✦ ✦ To Be Influenced by the Style of Others—Good Thing!

Something I have heard aspiring writers say that makes me shake my head in wonder is that they don't read much because they don't want to be influenced. They don't want their pure writing voice to be sullied. We should all hope to be so sullied.

Of all the ways to learn the craft of fiction, the greatest has to be reading. I don't even mean a concerted, targeted study of the great books. I mean reading in the normal sense, and the silent unconscious absorption of rhythm, tone, the ways of saying things that naturally occurs. I mean encountering words in a variety of contexts and discovering their connotations. This silent learning, filtered through ourselves, forms the base from which we will write—if we're lucky. None of us is smart enough or long-lived enough to replace the history of the development of literature with a solo intellectual act. To say you can do so is hubris and self-deception of a very high order. We have been surrounded by literature and its sounds since birth, whether anybody read to us or not, whether we read or not. The phrases of literature are everywhere, and we absorb them as surely as we absorb our parents' ways of speaking and the slang of our generation.

Beyond the unconscious absorption of styles from reading, I believe writers should consciously explore, imitate, and experiment with style. Why not? It's what painters do when trying to become painters, and they don't apologize for it. Try styles on like you would clothes, as part of how you acquire a facility in writing. Maybe it sounds bookish and nerdy, but that was one of my forms of play as a teenager. On a trip through the Rockies with my parents, a friend and I ignored the mountains in favour of writing naughty little paragraphs and dialogues, trying to one-up one another in the styles of our favourite authors. It was play, but it was part of how I went beyond silent understanding of how these writers wrote to some demonstration of their techniques on paper.

The natural question is: "What if, instead of writing like me, I wind up writing like the author I admire? What if I do and cannot stop?"

This happens. I won't deny it. It happened to me for a good part of my twenties when I was under the spell of J.P. Donleavy. It was a pleasant-enough spell to be under, but it didn't advance my writing—or did it? I undoubtedly learned some things I still use today. But as a dominating force in my writing, it was a phase, and it went away.

Eventually, after being stuffed with the styles of other writers for a decade, my style began to emerge. But all the experimentation under the thrall of others, and the learning of technique, was what allowed me to find my voice. If you don't have a facility with language, you cannot express your voice. You lack the tools.

It seems possible as well that if you arrive at your voice and style early, based on too little experience of literature and the world, it might not be as fine a voice or style as you might achieve if you gave yourself more time to absorb and evolve. This is a big generalization. If it seems to criticize those who publish early, then I need to add a sentence or two. Achievement isn't the point so much as stasis. If early achievement were to make a writer stop evolving, on the assumption that he or she has found a voice and it is the best voice, then that would be too bad. A person keeps changing throughout life, so why shouldn't literary style and voice change? Early success is wonderful, but it shouldn't be allowed to prevent development and improvement.

A fact worth remembering is that, even if you are writing under the influence of the styles of others, it doesn't mean that you won't publish. It doesn't mean that editors will sniff out the influence and toss you aside. I published a novel during my J.P. Donleavy period, and the only critic to comment on any stylistic similarity was one I had confessed to in advance. Either I was doing it so badly that it wasn't noticeable, or the critics of that day weren't as well read as they should have been.

As is probably obvious by now, I consider development of voice and style to be a lifelong business. I love to read early books by authors I admire. Their styles are usually there in some emerging way, as if visible at a depth through water. Through a series of books or stories, those styles attach more and more to themselves. They rise, clarify, and surface. Then they change to a different pool altogether, rise and surface again.

✦ ✦ ✦ What Is Style?

One way of answering this question is to say that style is what differentiates one writer from another. Someone in the business of analyzing literature might also declare it to be that which is similar among writers. Personally, I believe that the style of a work should be as much a function of the story or book, and especially of the characters, as it is a function of the author. Style arises out of the self, as illuminated by the world and other writing styles. It is profoundly cultural as well as personal. But the character in the story also has a culture, experience, and influences, which are likely not identical to those of the writer. Characters should have their say in the style by which they are represented.

A style is made up of a long list of things, and this chapter will deal with an important few. At its most basic, style is made of *diction* (the choice of words) and *syntax* (the way sentences are constructed). Style will also be looked at as a composite built of *rhythm, tone,* and *mood.* Sliced through from another direction, style is about *simplicity, complexity,* and *density.*

✦ ✦ ✦ Diction and Syntax

The choice of words and their organization into sentences lie at the heart of style. Beginning writers are often told they must learn to write simply and that a small word is always better than a bigger one. This advice can be good if it keeps a writer away from thinking that a pompous-sounding word is more arty and intelligent than a simple and direct one. But it is far from a pure truth. If a complex style expresses you or your story, or your point-of-view character, then to write simply would be terrible advice.

There is also a dangerous assumption that we should reserve a simple, minimal style for stories about people who are poor, uneducated, or rural. A good look at David Adams Richards's style in any of his novels about the Mirimachi River in New Brunswick will dispel that notion. His Giller Prize–winning *Mercy Among the Children* is about a poor and persecuted family, who happen to be well read. The novel shows that you can take on any subject, however cerebral, however literary, without violating the diction and syntax that is true to the characters.

The style of David Adams Richards's novels is incredibly complex. The sentences and paragraphs are built in dense, complex ways that represent the complicated business of perception and what's out there to be perceived, plus the dense complexity of the emotional and psychological life of the novel's people. Their lives are probably more complex than many middle-class lives, because they have so many trials and worries and conflicts and contradictions in their heads, brought on by difficult circumstance. It takes a layered and intricate style to represent them.

Simplicity in diction and syntax can mean something other than lack of complexity. Simplicity can be a good goal. We should always be looking for words that communicate our meaning most directly. "Canine" does not improve on "dog." "Collie" might improve on "dog" if that's what you want us to see; if it's important for us to know. In Greg Hollingshead's "The Dog in the Van," it was important that the dog be just a dog, nothing fancy, and so it was never called anything but a dog.

Following is a little example of writing that sins against simplicity in other ways:

She could not remember how she came to feel the way she did about the vase. There was certainly nothing unusual about it. A normal vase in all respects. But the vase did bother her and so she took it off the place where it had been and stored it away with several other things, in an area of the house she used for storing what had become unpleasant for her to see.

The purpose of this paragraph is to show how devious we can be and willing to not say what is there in a scene. In terms of sins against simplicity, it is long for its meaning. A sparse style might render it: *The vase annoyed her. She moved it.*

"A normal vase in all respects" says nothing about the vase. It lacks any hint of visual image. Even to say it is a black vase is an improvement. Why say "the place where it had been" if that place is a mantle? Why call it "an area of the house she used for storing" if that place is a closet under the stair closed off by a door? What are the "other things"? If they're not important, don't bring them up.

Simplicity, in this sense, can be all about directness and the visibility of the details presented. Often, when a writer does what I've done in the example, the choices may not be style choices at all, but a failure on the part of the writer to see the place and the vase and the other things in his or her own mind. The writer can be expressing his or her own vagueness, which produces a corresponding vagueness in readers.

If you look at Edna Alford's "Half-Past Eight" in terms of diction and syntax, you'll notice that most sentences move from subject through verb to object. They don't look back on themselves but are always propelling forward. Forward is where readers want to go. In terms of diction, Alford stays close to

Tessie's diction, because the sound of Tessie's voice is always with us. We are inside or close to her thoughts, and so it would make no sense to go outside her words and fish in someone else's diction pond.

At the same time, Alford is precise in the details presented: the bronze shimmer of the mirror, the dowager dresser with the ornate brass hooks, the "Scarlet Fire" lipstick. The style is crisp and visual. The sentences are not short and sharp and blunt, but fluidly long without seeming complex. That is, they are easy to read. They have a graceful ease. Look at the use of dashes by which she inserts an extra thought, or a related image, or example of what Tessie is talking about:

> And Mrs. Morrison wasn't much better—"Yes, Helen this" and "Yes, Helen that"—a spineless old bat if there ever was one.

If asked to sum up her style in this story, I would probably say that Edna Alford has perfect pitch for the inner voice of Tessie, and that her choice of diction and her syntax constructions never violate that fidelity to character. I would say that her consistent use of precise details, precisely modified, is cleverly achieved through Tessie, so that readers are given a sharp scene to experience and engage with, even when Tessie is alone.

At this same level of diction and syntax, look again at "The Dog in the Van." The style is simple, clear, and clean. What makes it so at the beginning is a series of declarations about the van and the dog: what the van looks like, what the dog looks like, what the Crossleys are doing that brings the dog into their path. You might call the style "rational," and that is the perfect style considering the point of view belongs to Dick Crossley, who prefers things clear, simple, and rational—uncomplicated. The dog in the van is the exact kind of complication he seeks to avoid.

Notice the last lines of the story's second paragraph, when instead of what Dick sees, we are for a few seconds transported into what Dick sees the dog seeing. The style changes, and so do the images when the dog's POV is presented: "a fly dying in the dust of the dashboard." The dog sees like an artist compared to Dick.

Character is almost entirely conveyed in this story through dialogue. Short bursts of words. "Dick! He's been shot." Through the dialogue, we learn how sympathetic and empathetic Jan naturally is—and how tight, argumentative, and unemotional Dick tries to be.

If asked to sum up the style of this story, on the basis of diction and syntax, I would stress how the simple descriptions in the crisp, rational sentences are the stylistic outgrowth of Dick's personality and a good example of how character and style are matched in a good story.

"The Dog in the Van" and "Half-Past Eight" both favour a fairly long sentence. In the Hollingshead story, sentences may begin with "when" or "if" subordinate clauses. In addition to the main clauses of sentences in "Half-Past Eight," phrases are often inserted inside commas or dashes. In the work of both authors, phrases are often added at the end, sometimes in lists like the list of things the dog sees inside its van.

The diction and syntax in "Stranger Than Fiction" are different from those in "The Dog in the Van" and Half-Past Eight." I submit off the top that it is because the point-of-view character is so different. Whereas Dick Crossley is tight and rational, and Tessie is direct and thoughtful, the author/narrator in Diane Schoemperlen's story is wild, loquacious, and humorous. If she were in the room with you, she would probably talk a mile a minute, frequently interrupt herself and you, and go off on tangents as new things popped into her head. She would make you laugh. Diane Schoemperlen uses a creative vocabulary in the story but not arcane or formal words. The author/narrator is made believable in part by her sounding like a fun neighbour dropping in to gossip and vent emotions. It is a deception as well, because whose neighbour would think to get off such memorable juggernauts of words as the story of the juggler at the East Azilda Fall Fair with which the story begins? But the cleverness is in the ideas. They are also cleverly worded, using a fund of vocabulary within all our experiences and not that different from our own.

The sentences in this story are often long, and that is part of how the narrator's breathlessness, her hurry, is achieved. She piles on new things, and the syntax rolls from one idea to another across the conjunction "and." This happened and then that happened, and then something else happened.

As in "Half-Past Eight," you'll notice how the details in "Stranger Than Fiction" are never general. The narrator sprays the reader with details. If you go to the early introduction of the first fictional Sheila, we hear about the meaning of her name, then her age, her figure, her eyes and hair—and by comparison, we hear about the author's hair, which is different. Then she moves on to Sheila's marital situation, her exercise habits ... It is fact, fact, fact, until she reaches the concluding paragraph of the description, which uses a metaphor, comparing Sheila and Roger's marriage to a pair of ice dancers.

✦ ✦ ✦ Rhythm

In "Stranger Than Fiction," Diane Schoemperlen builds rhythm by combining sentences across the conjunction "and." Instead of meeting the full stop of a period, the sentences are allowed to continue and mount up, with the result that there is a surging, galloping rhythm. In her case, the technique develops the author/narrator's breathless style. Other writers use the same technique to produce a different rhythm for different reasons. Short-story writer and novelist Alistair MacLeod, who is very well known for the rhythm of his work, does the same thing with sentences linked through "and," by which he produces an incantatory rhythm.

Other writers deliberately avoid anything like a long, lilting rhythm. Ernest Hemingway was perhaps the original revolutionary in this regard, often cutting his sentences to staccato lengths. His short words and sentences produced a curt, blunt style often used to describe blunt, violent events.

Much of what we're talking about here transgresses what we were taught was good grammar in school. When it comes to literary style, it is almost nonsense to talk about good English or obedience to one style guide or another. I remember being told that good style was mixing complex sentences with short sentences to produce a varied effect. I don't want to lampoon teachers who were just trying to open up these notions to a mind that did not contain them, but we should when we write as adults get over a lot of this advice. Alternating sentence lengths could be the worst of advice. It could produce a mechanical rhythm out of sync with your story.

If it's a cool grey day, write it in a cool grey way.

Canada, like many other countries, has enormous regional differences in how people speak, and one result is that the fictional work of Maritime writers, like Alistair MacLeod, David Adams Richards, Donna Morrissey, and Lynn Coady, is laced through with a rhythm you won't find in Prairie writing or West Coast writing. Nor should you. Dialect differences affecting rhythm are one of the beauties of literature, and I don't only mean the rhythms of Celtic-influenced writing or Caribbean-influenced writing. Beauty in literature is not as simple a thing as that, and the writing of other cultures not so evidently rhythmical has rhythm that the author can find and use to create.

A trick that can help you get a feel for fiction's rhythm is to hum it. Read it as if reading aloud but without articulating the words. Pause in the usual ways, and put the stresses where the writer meant them to be, but hum. You might hear the rhythm as distinct from the other effects and understand it in a stronger way. If that doesn't sound too loco, try it.

✦ ✦ ✦ Tone and Mood

Mood is the emotional quality of a passage of fiction. I imagine it like a colour overlay. You have events going on, thoughts, dialogue, but all with a blue or a red cast that is the emotion. A good example is how Rachel Wyatt manages to maintain the overlay or underlay of grief through the story "Visitation." (I won't elaborate on this point, as I want you to do so as an experiment at the end of this chapter.)

Tone is a psychological rather than an emotional quality. Think of sarcasm, for example. Sarcasm is not an emotion. In literature, sarcasm is, therefore, a tone rather than a mood.

To study what goes into the creation of mood, let's return to a concept mentioned in Chapter 6. You were asked to describe a man baking a cake in one mood and then in a different mood. Try it again with a room in your house or with your backyard. Write the description once as simple documentary. Then turn around and write it again from scratch when you as the writer are sad or angry or delighted, or the winner of a lottery, or tired from a night of torrid love-making. Try a variety of moods.

Afterward, examine what changed when you did this. Usually what changes is the details you seize on. Our whole connotative apparatus is at work, finding details it registers as sad-making, glad-making, mad-making, and so on.

Mood can be literally enhanced through colour. The Swedish director Ingmar Bergman in his movie *Nicholas and Alexandra* contrasted two families: one quiet and sinisterly depressed, the other wild, expressive, and joyful. The sad family was always awash in greys and pale blues. Everything at the happy family's house was saturated reds and gold. You probably could not get away with such gaudy artifice in fiction, but it does show how colour or lack of it can be used to convey moods.

Tone is even harder to talk about. Why is something sarcastic? Cutting? Depressing? Comforting? Sarcasm is often about irony, saying one thing when you mean another. Diane Schoemperlen is great for the study of tone because much of what she writes is tongue-in-cheek, with a wink, with irony—but delivered with a straight face. She lays out the examples of how life is stranger than fiction at the beginning of that story as if she were simply retelling a fact. The humour in the tone comes from its being more elaborate than what we have ever experienced, a burlesque satire of the usual little coincidences people insist are important.

If writers write, "Oh joy," they are seldom conveying joy. That is tone.

✦ ✦ ✦ Density

There are many wonderful metaphors to describe the art of fiction. The Edmonton writer Merna Summers has many wonderful metaphors to describe the art of fiction. One is to compare the writing of fiction to the dipping of a candle. Each pass thickens the candle: an image of how the quality of density is achieved in fiction. To some extent, writers do create density by the progressive addition of powerful details. That is, rather than adding new sentences and new paragraphs, they work new material into the existing sentences and paragraphs, adding to their weight and emotional, sensory complexity.

The effect on the reader is to be acted on by an increasing number of sensual and intellectual cues. You see more, hear more, feel more, and are surrounded by more hints and ideas. Hence, the experience becomes more complex. In terms of sound, the music of the prose becomes more intricate and, if well done, beautiful.

In Canadian literature, look at Mark Anthony Jarman's work for an example of this kind of density (the novel *Salvage King, Ya!* or the short-story collection *Nineteen Knives*), or at Zsuzsi Gartner's short-story collection *All the Anxious Girls on Earth*. Malcolm Lowry's *Under the Volcano* is a unique model of style density.

Other writers will choose deliberately not to produce such a density because it doesn't suit their story. Dense fictional style slows down time, allows us to get within a moment and experience it on many levels, hyper-realistically. Another writer's purpose might be to speed time up through a loose, sparse style. Or fidelity to the character might demand a less frenetic, hypersensual treatment; for example, the opening makeup scene in "Half-Past Eight." Time is slowed, the detail is dense, but it is limited to what Tessie is doing and thinking now.

Another style alternative is minimalism. Probably no writer is more associated with minimalism in fiction than Raymond Carver. By deliberately choosing only a few strong details for a scene, Carver achieved terrific impact. Dialogue in his work is likewise bare and blunt. This is hyper-realism again, but achieved in the opposite way to the progressive addition of detail. In Carver's short stories, the few perfectly chosen details land like blows. Because of the lack of competition from many other details, each one has maximum impact. In his dialogue, the reader strains to dig out the meaning of the cryptic messages.

Carver's minimalism was a powerful influence on a generation of writers, though many who followed his artistic lead have since re-inflated their styles. Going back to my original thoughts on experimentation with style, by all means read and be influenced by Raymond Carver. It looks so easy and is so difficult to do.

Another category of style is humour. What makes a story humorous? How does the humorous stylist achieve what he or she does? This is a big topic, popular with writers, and I've devoted a good deal of my career to it. It is the subject of the chapter to come.

✦ ✦ ✦ Your Process

"Visitation" was not used as a source of examples in this chapter. That is because I wanted you to write a style synopsis of "Visitation," of the kind done in the previous chapter for other stories.

- How does Rachel Wyatt manage to create and maintain the mood of grief in the story?

- How is the humorous tone brought in?

- Talk about how diction and syntax obey Almeida's character and also help define that character for readers.

- How does the style suit the story?

- Can you imagine another style in which the story might have been written?

- Redo the exercise of describing a place or person, and then writing it again when you are angry, sad, joyful, and so on. Do it a couple of times and then evaluate how the change in mood and tone was created, from the plain version to the emotionally flavoured one.

- For the next chapter, read "Positive Images" by Fred Stenson.

... *Positive Images*

a short story by **FRED STENSON**

I lost my first tooth to hockey in the middle of my fourth NHL season, and being the kind of fierce competitor that I am, I said: that's it, I quit. I was fond of and proud of my teeth. I counted on them to assist me in some lucrative hockey afterlife. Most of all, I counted on them to help me attract a woman before I left hockey and lost the only edge I have. But there it was: at the end of a lopsided game in Montreal, in the time it takes to lose a draw, a twenty-two-year-old maniac had driven his helmet into my mouth and disfigured me for life.

That same night, I phoned my agent, Bernie. Through a mouthful of blood-soaked cotton batting, I told him of my decision to leave hockey. I thought I was ready for anything he might throw at me but the bastard tricked me. He cried.

For some unaccountable reason, perhaps that I was in mourning over the recent death in my mouth and near tears myself, Bernie's crying touched me deeply — much more, for example, than when he said, "After all that I've done for you, Burns." I honestly couldn't think what that might be. Taking a greedy cut of my salary didn't seem particularly heroic. Then I decided he must mean the only endorsement contract he'd ever negotiated on my behalf: a TV spotlight for Uniglobe, a manufacturer of athletic supporters and cans.

The first image in the commercial was a defenceman wearing a Lone Ranger mask, winding up in slow motion for a slap shot. At the top of his wind-up, real motion kicks in and he smashes the puck toward the camera. The screen goes black. The sound of broken glass. Cut to me in a suit, standing in front of an empty net, holding the contraption on the palm of my hand. "Uniglobe," I say. "Believe me, it makes a difference."

Besides a modest amount of quickly spent cash, this television appearance gained me a nickname. That's right: "Glass Balls." Worse still, part of my contract was that I had to wear a Uniglobe for the whole season. It had a lot of snaps and straps and, when it was on, it looked like a lady's garter belt. In the heat of play, the snaps came unfastened and, back on the bench, I spent most of my time working it back up my hockey sock. This caused trouble with the TV station that broadcast our home games. "Every time we cut to your bench," they said, "Burns is playing with himself."

But the night of the loss of my tooth, Bernie's tears over the telephone sawed through my resolve and on down through all the things I held against him. These whimpers and snorts made a lot more sense two years later when Bernie was busted at the Toronto airport for a large bag of white stuff taped into his armpit. After his conviction, he revealed all in hopes of getting a book out of it. Referring back to the time of our telephone conversation, he claimed his habit was topping two thousand dollars a week.

I knew nothing of this at the time. I just thought Bernie had bad sinuses and a rare case of moustache dandruff and, in this precise moment, was all torn up to think that our business friendship was over. Feeling myself slipping, I trotted out the line I'd been rehearsing all evening.

"A missing tooth is a hole in your head for life, Bernie."

There was a loud double snort on the line. "And a million out of your wallet is a hole in your head since birth."

I bit. "What million?"

"The million I can get you over two seasons."

"Hold on. You mean four." My current salary was $270,000. While it was true the team was keen to renegotiate my contract, an upward direction in the salary figure wasn't what they had in mind.

"No!" More coughs and splutters. Poor guy, I thought. Broken heart. "Two. Three tops."

"What do you know, Bernie?"

"I've had my ear to the ice, okay?" More like his nose in the snow. "Trust me."

Trust an agent. Weird notion.

"There's no way, Bernie. Mr. Topworth can't afford it."

"Who says Topworth will own the team next year? Who says the team will even be in the same city? That's all I'm saying, Burns. Don't be a fool."

So was I a fool? Did I quit hockey the night of the violent appearance of a gap in my smile? No, I did not. But the reasons had nothing to do with Bernie or with money, and very little to do with hockey. The simple truth was that, as I lay in bed that night, a mouth full of pain and unable to sleep, I was set upon by visions of myself in the life I would lead outside of hockey. I saw myself in a predictable assortment of menial jobs and I saw myself always alone, alone and wishing I had stayed in hockey long enough to find a wife.

Whatever my opinion of hockey as a sport, I have always respected it as a means of getting homely, dull-witted men superior wives. The undeniable proof had come the previous summer when I was called upon to stand at the side of my cornerman Smitty Smith, and to hand him a ring which he tried to jam onto the wrong finger of a young woman named Pearl. Now, it's not up to me to say what Pearl wasn't; but she was the reasonably attractive hostess of a rib joint where Smitty regularly reduced the equivalent of a yearling steer to a pile of bones on his plate. She did manage to read a romance novel every two weeks. And once, when Smitty miscounted his bill by twenty or so dollars, she did pursue him into the parking lot and demand restitution.

And there she was, suddenly united in matrimony to a man, who, when signing the register after his vows, looked like he was trying to part the facets of a diamond with a pickaxe.

Smitty, married. And yet, there I stood beside him, rather dapper in my tuxedo, almost handsome and unmarked as hockey players go — and single. Woefully single.

In all those seasons of nights of sitting in bars replacing fluids after games, when women would gather and pairings were made, I could never seem to strike the right balance. Burke, our captain, noticing how I always turned women away or was turned away by them, offered this advice: "You always think you're too good, Burns, except when you think you're not good enough." This, from no Rhodes Scholar, was true.

Eight times out of ten, a woman leaning my way would do something or say something that put me totally off. It could be so small: reaching down and making a sound of fingernail on nylon that I couldn't bear; or saying that I reminded her of a movie star and, pressed for details, naming some jerk I disliked; or just a mention of some other hockey player she had "known." Virginity isn't a big issue with me but the idea of another hockey player, some empty-mouthed, scarred behemoth … it didn't bear thinking about then and it doesn't now.

I said eight out of ten times were like that. Number nine was the result of my standing around expensive hotel lobbies striking what I thought were intriguing, man-of-the-world poses. This worked for James Bond and it worked for me too. Often a woman would appear by my side, asking for a light or some such conversation starter. In my best James Bond style, I would compliment her loveliness and suggest a drink after the game (thus working in that I was a professional hockey player). And every damn time this happened, later, in the intimacy of her room, she would turn out to be a call girl.

No matter how much I spent on clothes and hair stylists, no matter how hard I practised my poses in front of the bathroom mirror, there was just no fooling these ladies. They could spot a fat wallet on a farm boy's hip through any get-up, at any distance. Alas, I was not nearly as good at spotting them and, time after time, I'd wind up in a hotel room shelling out her atrociously high fee for nothing.

Now if that sounds like a lie, consider how hard I have worked in the heat of the hockey wars to keep my good health and looks. No condom in the world is thick enough to console my fear of sexually transmitted, incurable disease. And because I always felt it was my fault, not theirs, I always paid. If their professional ethics demanded they do something for me in return, I'd request a backrub and "no funny stuff." During this backrub, I would often tell about my pining search for a wife, my desperate belief that pro hockey would help me find one. It owed me that much at least.

The tenth time was the woman I admired. A woman who did nothing to repel me and much to attract me; who, to my knowledge, had never met a hockey player before; who was as frightened of sex with strangers as I was. As Burke put it: the woman for whom I felt not good enough. When such a rare woman came within range of my wooing, I would do one of two things: I would slink away in a fit of sulking self-pity, or I would fawn (which, defined by the Oxford Dictionary, means "trying to win attention or affection by crouching close and trying to lick"). And, while fawning, I would make a funny sound scratching a bruise through my trouser leg, or I would tell her she looked like a movie star and, when pressed, would name the wrong one. If she didn't feel she was too good for me at the outset, I wouldn't let up until she did.

All this came to me in the sleepless night after the loss of my tooth and, by dawn, I had decided I couldn't quit hockey, not yet. I would wait until the end of the season and, given that the Bisons were once again virtually out of the playoffs by midseason, that meant I had exactly thirty-eight games to change my luck and find a woman to admire who could admire me back.

When thirty-eight games had dwindled down to twenty, my dignity crumbled. I phoned Helmet Soffshel, who was listed in the Yellow Pages as a professional publicist. I told him I wanted to throw a party for myself in the penthouse suite of the city's grandest hotel.

"But what's the occasion?" Helmet kept asking. "There must be an occasion."

"It's the occasion of my desperately needing a wife," I told him.

"Ooh, pathetic," he said. "That won't do at all."

On this point I agreed with Helmet and it was to give the party a respectable purpose that I publicly admitted my plan to retire. The party became my preretirement bash, my paean of praise to the game of my life.

Everything had to be paid for in advance: caviar, canapés, champagne, a tasteful, three-piece jazz ensemble, napkins and matchbooks with my name and career-span specially printed on, a battalion of black-tie waiters, a good-looking hostess. To be honest, when I got a load of Renata, the hostess, a striking Cleopatra with hair like spun coal, I almost asked her to marry me on the spot. If she had happened by some miracle to say yes, I could have reached my goal at a fraction of the cost. Between Renata and Helmet, my bank account had begun to make a noise like an aircraft toilet flushing.

"But will there be women?" I nagged Helmet whenever he served me with a fresh passel of bills. He didn't strike me as having a lot of experience in that regard.

"I'm working on it," he'd say and I never cared for the struggle this implied.

Helmet insisted that I must not be visible for the first half hour of my party. I stayed in the back bedroom in a ridiculously overgroomed state, standing arms out like a scarecrow so as not to tax my deodorant. I also looked in all the drawers for a Bible but apparently Gideons don't do penthouse suites. One of my odd habits in those days was to read the last book of the Bible whenever I was in a hotel room. The part about the end of the world spoke to me personally.

Without biblical assistance that night, I had to content myself with apocalyptic daydreams. Four horses on skates breathed fire and other kinds of warming corruption on the world until they had it completely melted, including both polar ice caps. All of creation drowned except for a handful of goats and a few Sherpas, the latter setting out immediately to build an ark of *krumholz*. What they should have been building were skates. After the apocalypse, the world cooled off rapidly. It cooled, it froze; it became a uniform sphere of gleaming ice.

"Okay, Dougie, let's go."

Helmet stood in the bedroom doorway, in a crimson tuxedo and royal purple cummerbund. He beckoned me into the party room. Confetti and streamers flew; the band kicked into a tasteful rendition of "For He's Jolly Good Fellow." Just before I was blinded by flashbulbs, which presumably I was also paying for, I saw enough to sink my hopes titanically. In the blue and orange blindness that followed, an item in one of Helmet's recent ledgers pulsed in neon: "Guests - $2,000." When my vision cleared, I went around the room greeting my teammates, their superior wives, a few reporters — and a reunion of local and regional call girls, many of whom had given me expert and expensive backrubs.

In its way it was a nice party and, at times, dancing with the call girls or the superior wives, I felt little surges of sentimentality for the game I was leaving. When Smitty felt compelled to dump the ice and fruit from an empty punch bowl over my head, I laughed. A few minutes later I undid his suspenders at the back and pulled down his trousers to reveal his boxer shorts with the cartoons, front and back. It was fun but, at the end of the night, when the guests paraded past me at the door, my mood was plunging past all previously known lower horizons.

When the last guest had gone, I turned and faced the dismantling of my dreams for the evening. Helmet was marshalling the serving crew for a cleanup of empty glasses and plates; the band members were storing their equipment away into black cases; and Renata, the hostess, was approaching me with a slip of paper in her hand; Renata, beautiful, stoic, emotionally featureless, to whom the clockwork efficiency of the party owed so much.

Seeing the slip of paper, I reached automatically for my wallet.

"A success?" she asked crisply.

"No," I answered, too depressed to worry about it's being an insult to her craft.

"You didn't find a woman."

I wanted at that moment to pull off Helmet's cummerbund with such force that he spun a hole through all twenty-nine floors of the building.

"Of course I knew," she said. "I had to."

"I didn't meet anyone."

"Yes, you did."

And she poked the slip of paper into my jacket pocket, right on top of my red silk puff handkerchief.

Yes, the note on top of my puff handkerchief contained Renata's full name, address and phone number. It was significant that the data was handwritten on paper rather than machine-printed on a business card. That very evening, Renata had decided to marry me, subject to a review of my assets.

Because I was busy with a writing project and Renata was enrolled in one of those deep immersion "How To Make A Million" courses, our wedding didn't take place until two months after the end of the season. Smitty had a particularly long and snorty laughing fit during the ceremony and the severe lady Justice of the Peace had to interrupt her recitation twice while the old cornerman got a hold of himself.

I can't really remember anything else — except for one thing. I remember the part of the wedding involving the ring. First, Smitty had some trouble getting the ring box out of his trouser pocket. He tickled himself to more laughter in the process. I opened the blue box myself because he didn't realize he was supposed to. Taking the wedding band, I swivelled to where Renata's finger was waiting. At that precise instant, I hesitated, not because I was having second thoughts but because the engagement ring already there on her finger looked unfamiliar. I could not recognize it at all. I'd been there for the purchase, a peripheral figure with a chequebook while Renata and the salesperson talked carats and facets, and I did have a good look at the ring while shelling out the megabucks. I didn't mention this, of course, and I slipped the wedding band on beside it dainty as can be. Then I snapped Renata a worried look. I was afraid I would see a stranger's face inside the veil.

We honeymooned in Vegas and had our first argument when Renata wanted to see Wayne Newton and I wanted to see an illusionist who claimed he could cut an elephant into thirds. Renata couldn't wait to get home. When we did return, she transformed into something you'd need high technology equipment to photograph. My eyes weren't up to the test and what I remember of the ensuing months is a series of blurs: a blurred figure rolling on blurred stockings and applying blurred makeup in front of the bedroom mirror of a house so new and strange it scared me every morning; blurred lips at the telephone while I waited on my side of the bed pretending to read *Esquire*.

To use the management phrase, Renata put my money to work. Me too. Besides buying as much real estate as my money could mortgage, she attached my still-recognizable name to every worthy cause in the city. When she left the bedroom and the house each day, and my head cleared of the blur of her, I would find a list on the bedside table. I never saw her make this list but it was always there. Place, time, contact person, cause, suggested dress, and in quotation marks, a sentence she wanted me to say. "A progressive zoo is one of the most valuable institutions a city can have." "Integration of the handicapped into the mainstream of society is one of the most important challenges facing us today." I lived in fear of mixing them up.

The closest moment I ever came to seeing Renata still in those days was a moment in our kitchen in the eighth month of marriage. I came out in my bathrobe to find her, amazingly, still there at 9:00AM. The still moment was the pause before she said, "Doug, you're no longer bankable." It is important to record that she said this without accusation or pity; more in the way you might say, "The milk company no longer delivers." She went on to say that she was staging me out of the worthy cause business and that I had a choice: I could have an office and a meaningless job in her growing empire, or I could do nothing. I told her I thought nothing was more my line.

Nothing. How extraordinarily difficult it is to do. In my opinion, doing nothing is a worthy cause and one of the greatest challenges facing our society today. I don't think anyone does it very well.

So I failed at doing nothing and, after I failed, I had a breakdown. At least that's what Renata said I had. What happened was that I went stealthily about finding out what assets and savings plans were still in my name. For some mysterious tax reason, several things were. The house I had never thought of as anything but Renata's house turned out to be mine.

I went to a bank with paper evidence of my collateral and I told them I wanted to start a chain of doughnut shops. When asked what experience I had, I told them I was an ex-professional hockey player just like the late Tim Horton. The bank's loans manager was very uppity but, when enough earthly chattels had been piled opposite the transaction, the loan was approved.

Many would not view what came next as a success but I do. After months of secret preparations, I opened the three flagships of what I dreamt would soon become a national navy of doughnut outlets. I insisted that the "Opening Soon" banner be dropped at a carefully synchronized instant. Suddenly, there it was, my secret, my pride, revealed to the world.

DOUGIE BURNS DOUGHNUTS

The equipment was primed. Miles of doughnut dough hit the boiling fat. They were good tasting little devils, too. It wasn't until far too late that it occurred to me that *Burns* is a word that should never appear side-by-side with *doughnut*.

People can say what they like about Renata but I think she behaved very decently that day and right through to the end. In the evening of that quiet opening day, Renata came into my best location, the downtown one, looking splendid in a black suit and blue satin blouse. I remember being grateful that she had left her briefcase in the car. She sat opposite me across a crumb-strewn, doughnut-coloured formica table. I don't think you can surprise Renata and she did not look surprised that night. She looked efficient, like a surgical nurse, and she efficiently told me that no one was going to eat a potentially charred foodstuff, that I had had a breakdown, and that she would stand by me through my period of recovery. She had already booked me into a "resort" in Oregon that specialized in whatever I had.

Despite being there for several months, I don't feel like an authority on the resort that became my next home. If I'm pinned down, I say that broken lives were mended there through the medium of golf. Like most hockey players, I was a better than average golfer already but Skip, my pro at the resort, took several strokes off my score by correctly analyzing the mechanics of my slice and through what he called "positive imaging."

"If you can see yourself hit the ball straight, Dougie, you can hit the ball straight."

Skip said this once a hole and we must have played five thousand holes.

Renata visited every month, on the same day each month, and I looked forward to seeing her even though the visits were pretexts to have me sign things. Early on, I signed papers pertaining to my personal bankruptcy and, later, the papers had to do with our divorce. On her last visit before I was released, she came with two lawyers, one for each of us, and mine took me outside near the first tee and read me the separation agreement. I almost wept at its contents. Renata was leaving me my favourite car and an amount of cash roughly equal to the investment funds she had gained by marrying me. What integrity. What a woman.

I hope people won't think this is a depressing story. I can only relate how I felt the day I left the resort in Oregon. Skip was there with my bags and clubs, helping me get them into my sports car, and he was joking about golf and positive imaging up a storm. I was not feeling as positive as I might have right then because I badly needed a drink. Most folks at the resort were alcoholics and, though never much of a drinker myself, I'd become fond of the adolescent ritual of sneaking out into the bushes each night to drink from their hidden bottles. By the time I was leaving, I had the pencilled outlines of my first and only addiction to alcohol.

The bags and clubs were in the car; the top was up against a light drizzle. Skip was grinning and proclaiming it a beautiful day. I believe he was glad it was raining because that made finding beauty in it a harder positive image to attain. I was shaking his hand, licking dry lips and wondering what in hell I was going to do now. I will never know if this was part of the intended process of my recovery or not but, at that exact instant, a hugely positive good feeling powered through me and burst, drenching me in a shower of itself.

Then I was driving away, down the tree-lined dripping drive. Skip was waving with both hands, a shrinking photograph in my rearview. And I was surging and glowing with all this positive happiness. I'm only twenty-seven, I kept telling myself. Already in this life I have been an NHL hockey player; I've been married to a beautiful woman; I've been an entrepreneur. I've had a bankruptcy, a divorce and a breakdown. I've lost a tooth in a hockey punchup and had it replaced with one almost as good. I'm really living, I told myself, and I knew it was true.

At the stop sign before the Interstate, I confidently signalled left. I drove to the Canadian border. Brimming with positive happiness, I drove home.

• • •

...*II*

Humorous Fiction

ECCENTRICS, MISFITS, ORDINARY PEOPLE

TAKEN BY SURPRISE

When serving as a mentor for beginning writers burning with desire to write humour, I try to send them down that appealing but lonely road without too much of a burden of negative advice. What good would it do to rain on their parade by telling them that humorous fiction in Canada is a ghetto, with its one little prize named for wonderful Stephen Leacock, and given as often as not to someone whose work would have made him cringe long before it ever made him laugh? Why say how much smarter it is to write fiction that happens to be funny in places but is serious overall (for then you might fool readers into letting you out of humour's ghetto to play with the big boys and girls)? People who are hot to destroy their readers with laughter will seldom listen to such cautions anyway.

What I hope they would listen to is advice about how to *be* funny in fiction, and that's what this chapter is all about.

Lectures on humorous writing often begin with a steely-eyed, not-very-amusing-looking person staring at you with doubt and saying, "First: you must be funny." Any way you look at it, being funny *is* a prerequisite. If people seem to find your verbal anecdotes and asides worth laughing at, that's a good sign. But it's not a guarantee, any more than the absence of these responses guarantees the impossibility of your ever being funny in print. The people in ordinary life who get the most credit for being funny are those who work at it hardest, who perform most easily and uninhibitedly, and who laugh at their own jokes. Quieter sorts are thought not to be funny, when that has nothing to do with sense of humour at all. I've often read to an audience, with a strong response of laughter, only to have someone who "knows" me come up afterward and say, "I never guessed you were funny." It's a compliment of a sort.

Being funny in fiction is different than being funny in life. There may be a total overlap and there may not be; therefore, I invite those who think they would like to write humorous fiction to give it a try. The world, being cruel, will let them know if the experiment fails.

Another thing to get out of the way at the outset is the question of whether being funny can be taught. Like any other human ability or talent, it cannot be created through teaching, but it can be improved. Another expectation I would like to blunt is any assumption that this chapter on humour will itself be funny. Humour is serious business to me. I approach it with dour mien.

This discussion of humour will be illustrated with reference to Rachel Wyatt's "Visitation," Diane Schoemperlen's "Stranger Than Fiction," and my short story "Positive Images."

◆ ◆ ◆ **The Protagonist's Problem**

Imagine a spectrum of humorous fiction. On one end is fiction whose entire intention is to be funny. On the other end is fiction that is tragic but still contains humour. All the other possible intentions, involving humour in fiction, lie in-between.

Rachel Wyatt's "Visitation" is about as close to the tragic end of this spectrum as I can imagine. What could be more tragic than the death of someone's child? But the story is nonetheless humorous, when cartoonish cousin Martha comes to call, with her grief ranch and her theories about what to feed the grief-stricken.

The first rule of writing humorous fiction has to be knowing what type you're trying to write. Is it a serious story that happens to be funny? Or is it a funny story that happens to be serious? Is it funny and serious in equal measure? If it is neither funny nor serious, throw it out.

For my money, the hardest thing to attempt, and I never do, is the story that is entirely funny: first sentence to last. Such a story rarely works, maybe never, not always because its jokes fail, but because the reader has no real reason to go on. Without a serious human story to propel the reader forward, it's just a joke book. Does it matter in a joke book whether you stop at page one or three or read to the end? Also, something that proclaims itself to be roaringly funny, that seems to be saying, "This is really going to crack you up," courts reader backlash. Readers look fiercely back and say, "Is it? Am I?" If the readers aren't with you, they are against you.

My number one rule about humour in short fiction is that the humorous short story protagonist needs to have a serious problem, every bit as much as the serious fiction protagonist. The protagonist needs to feel real pain. That is, the problem may be funny to readers, but *it can't be funny to the protagonist*. Readers read on, engage with the story in search of the problem's solution, just as they do in a serious story. The fact that the story is funny is almost incidental. The serious problem is what is providing the propulsion forward.

"Positive Images" is a short story of mine from a collection called *Teeth*. It is a linked collection about a fictional professional hockey team and its reluctant scoring star, Doug Burns. My master plan was to have every story somehow grow out of the same moment of climax in the first story when Doug Burns loses his first tooth to hockey in his fourth year as a pro.

This climax in the title story becomes the point of attack in "Positive Images." Doug has lost a tooth to hockey, and now he wants to retire. But, he realizes, on sober second thought, that he can't leave pro hockey until it yields him a superior wife. All his toothless teammates, the undeserving bunch, already have superior wives, and he wants one too. So Doug embarks on a systematic plan to find a wife, and the quest is the point of the story. The way the quest leads to his retirement party at season's end is the story's part one. The party is the big scene in part one, its climax, and as it winds down, it appears that Doug has failed. It appears that he has found no future wife. Then Renata, the party's hired hostess, comes over to him and begins a relationship that will lead (in part two) to their marriage.

The second part of the story, almost a second story, begins with Doug's marriage to Renata. They get married (the point of attack in part two), and Renata starts a number of successful business ventures with Doug's money. He hardly ever sees her. To try to keep pace, and to give meaning to his consort existence, Doug starts a chain of doughnut shops that are a failure from the moment their doors open. Renata's view of it, which Doug accepts, is that the doughnut chain's failure signifies that Doug has had a breakdown. To deal with it, Renata sends Doug to a spa that treats the fragile mind with heavy doses of golf. While he's there, she sends a lawyer to serve him with divorce papers.

Instead of another action climax, this story ends with Doug's new understanding of himself. As he's leaving the golf farm, where he has been healing with several rounds a day and lots of positive imaging, he realizes it has worked, something he never considered possible. "Positive imaging like mad," he begins to see his trials and troubles as a rich and varied life, and he continues on to his next adventure in a state of optimism.

In its two parts, Doug has at least two problems. He takes them seriously. If readers were to doubt his desire, his need, to have a wife, his fear of not getting one, the story would fail. Then, when he has a wife, and hardly ever sees her, his loneliness is again real. He feels it, and so should the reader. When Doug's doughnut shop fails, and he loses his wife, he is sad again. At the end, when Doug blossoms forth into freedom with a new optimism, I wanted readers to feel that joy.

The story illustrates a few other things about humorous fiction. Whatever the difference is between serious and humorous, it is not structural. This story has the same need for a point of attack and a build-up and a big scene and a meaningful end as a serious story. Whatever the difference is, structure's not it.

✦ ✦ ✦ The Big Scene

Although I'm not proposing it as a dogma, I have noticed in analyzing my humorous short stories that many of them have a big chaotic scene as a moment of climax. The party in "Positive Images" at the end of part one is an example. In the title story of the *Teeth* collection, the big scene is the hockey brawl in which Doug loses his tooth. Because the stories are meant to be funny, the big scenes have an element of burlesque. If I had been portraying a hockey brawl in a serious story, it would have been real blood and pain and smashed teeth and expletives undeleted—something sad, pathetic, and brutal. But in the burlesque version in "Teeth," I portray it like a big dance, where everyone has a dancing partner but Doug, who daydreams along the bench about an old girl-friend and a poignant post-pubescent moment. Just then, a young Montreal Canadien, frantic to find someone to hit, hunts Doug down. He smacks his head into Doug's mouth—and when I read it to an audience, the laughter stops right there. A respectful silence comes as Doug is helped off by the trainer.

People laugh at the burlesque because it is different from the real, because they are surprised. But the moment of violence, the banging out of the tooth, is serious. They like Doug. They don't want to see him maimed.

✦ ✦ ✦ The Ending

In the earlier discussion of short-story structure, the ending beyond the big scene, after the moment of revelation or the climax, was seen as a moody time when the emotions of the story reverberate. Another strong opinion I have about humorous short fiction is that if you have a big, bang-up burlesque scene for the climax, the audience is done laughing when that scene is finished. Whatever the other dominant emotion of the story is, besides humour, I go to that emotion for the story's ending.

In "Teeth," the burlesque scene of the hockey brawl that costs Doug a tooth is followed by a little scene of Doug in the locker room. Beyond humour, the other emotions in "Teeth" are Doug's fatigue with hockey, his desire to get out of it in one piece, his feeling of being trapped. At the end, I go to those emotions. If I have done it right, the mood should be bittersweet:

On the narrow bench in the dressing room. Mouth wadded full of cotton batting. The muffled roar of the crowd as the game peters out to its lop-sided conclusion.

The game ends. The team trudges in. Chip follows, raving about a shake-up. I am not around to be raved at, however. I am off in the near future this time, rather than the distant past I so often visit. In this near future, there are sticks but they are embedded in weenies and the soft bellies of ice-cream bars. There are pucks too, of bacon. Body checks come annu-ally at the doctor's office and he always pronounces you in great physical condition.

Somehow, every time I lick up under my swollen lip, I am reminded of this near future and the many sources from which money can come. Money, unlike teeth, can be replen-ished. A missing tooth is a hole in your head for life.

There is a saying that laughter and tears are close relatives. The success of a bittersweet ending to a humorous story depends on that truth—might even be proof of it. One of the greatest humorous novels I have ever read is J.P. Donleavy's *The Ginger Man*. It is a black comedy, ribald, a little nasty, often wildly funny. If you have not read it, or even if you have, have a look at the ending. It is wonderfully sad.

✦ ✦ ✦ Beginnings

Humorous story beginnings share with other fictional beginnings the need to hook the reader, but often the humorist will do so with a funny line or couple of lines. Remember the opening of "Stranger Than Fiction," or better, go back and look:

> *Aunt Maude was frightened by a bald albino juggler at the East Azilda Fall Fair when she was six months' pregnant …*

Schoemperlen's representation of people's stories about cosmic coincidences they claim to have witnessed or heard from reliable sources made me laugh.

In "Positive Images," I knitted together a point of attack, a startling statement, and what I hoped was a funny statement:

> *I lost my first tooth to hockey in the middle of my fourth season in the NHL, and, being the kind of fierce competitor that I am, I said, that's it, I quit.*

I believe a story that is going to be funny should tip you off in its first lines or page that this is the case. If a story begins tragically and then delivers humour, readers feel cheated—but not as cheated as if a story that started out as a rousing comedy turns tragic. For all its comedy, you will recall that "Visitation" begins with a sentence of utter sadness.

> Almeida went to answer the door hoping it was a stranger come to tell her that it had all been a mistake. *Mrs. Kerwell. Your child is alive and well and will be home tomorrow.*

Another hindsight discovery I have made about my own humorous writing is that my story protagonists fall into two camps: the eccentrics and the normals. Whenever I have built a story around an eccentric (such as Doug Burns, the hockey player), the comic plot consists of taking him and placing him in the situation that most conflicts with his eccentricities. In Doug's case, I put him in the game of professional hockey. Hockey players are said to be rough and tough, to play through pain, to be brave and foolhardy about their health. Doug is meek and frightened, and he would never play while in pain. He is cowardly and careful, and fanatical about his health and appearance. He is a misfit in this situation, and from this misfittedness flows the humour.

The eccentrics can be subcategorized as likeable, unlikeable, or blackly humorous. Doug Burns serves well enough as an example of the likeable eccentric, as does Diane Schoemperlen's author/protagonist in "Stranger Than Fiction."

For the second type, the unlikeable protagonist, "unlikeable" is a bit of a misnomer in that you generally do like the unlikeable protagonist; you just feel that perhaps you shouldn't. I have in mind J.P. Donleavy's Sebastian in *The Ginger Man*. You like him despite his doing some fairly unkind acts, such as cheating on his wife and refusing her money he intends to spend on drinking. Push it up another notch, and you have the black-humorous hero-villains, like Harry Flashman in George McDonald Fraser's *Flashman* novel series. Harry is a horrible guy. There is nothing he won't do to save himself; no vile lie he won't stoop to telling; no one he won't sacrifice. We read on in guilty fascination.

These eccentrics are also rendered misfits by the situations their authors put them in. Sebastian, a most unreliable and unhandy man, with a taste for high living, is placed in a marriage with an infant child in a poverty-stricken part of Dublin, in a flat with bad plumbing his wife would like to see him fix. Harry Flashman, a total coward, is put in the British army, and he is then made a British war hero by mistake. He must continually deal with the dangerous circumstances into which Britain's war-hungry government thrusts him.

The second type of protagonist I use for my humorous stories is the so-called normal or ordinary person. Again, the method of achieving the humour is by putting such people in situations that render them misfits. In a story called "Blueballs the Pirate," from a collection called *Working Without a Laugh Track*, I start with a fellow who prides himself on being an everyman. He lives in suburbia, has a nice wife and family, and brags of being totally satisfied. He goes off to his job that he enjoys, and he likes his co-workers with whom he shares many a merry joke. He would hate to be thought of as different.

Then he has a vasectomy by local anaesthetic.

He is so shocked by the experience and by the pain that comes later, and is so angry that no one warned him, that he undergoes a temporary personality change. He becomes the inverse of himself. He hates his wife and the restrictiveness of his marriage, his job, his life. He decides that he is running off to the Caribbean with the West Indian nurse who attended his surgery. He turns back into his ordinary self at the end, but he is haunted by the presence of that other dangerous fellow who inhabited him for a day.

In another story from the same collection, "Bill's Sperm Count," Bill, who has a nice marriage and an ordinary happy life, discovers himself unable to go through with giving a sperm sample at an infertility clinic. He keeps trying to overcome the obstacle, keeps failing, until it becomes a serious problem in his marriage. The ordinary man is again rendered a misfit by unexpected circumstance.

◆ ◆ ◆ **Voice in Humorous Fiction**

Voice may be the aspect of humorous fiction that is most often misunderstood. Nothing grates so much as when a writer puts on a funny voice to write a funny story. Might as well put on a funny hat. Often, these are high-tone voices jam-packed with jawbreaker words. Saying someone is astronomically stupid, saying someone is gargantuanly fat are not funny statements. Fat does not become hilarious by growth into the gargantuan, nor is stupidity funny just because you say it achieves astronomical proportions.

The adverb, for my money the most suspect part of speech, is often used by writers attempting to inflate the language as a means of achieving humour. The following example will try to combine the sins of elevated language, useless adverbs, and the funny-punny name.

> *Georgio Pantaloon sat up to the table as close as his voluminous abdomen would allow. He addressed his wife floridly while dashingly raising the silver soup spoon to his flabby, lubbering lips. "Soup's off, love. No crime. Just telling you," he added simperingly.*

My reaction to something like this is as Rachel Wyatt writes in "Visitation": *Why not the rack, oh Lord! Why not a plague of frogs!*

The voice in third-person short fiction (humour included) should be heavily influenced by the point-of-view character it represents. In first-person fiction, it simply is that person. Characters in humour are often eccentric. The form of their eccentricity may be an odd rhetorical style, an intriguing turn of phrase, a penchant for exaggeration. Whatever it is, it is correct for this eccentricity to enter and guide the voice of the story. It is right because it originates not in the mind of the author, but in the mind of the character.

If instead we look at the other type of protagonist, the normal or ordinary person, why would that person have an odd, intriguing, or unique style of address? As pointed out in an earlier chapter, even neutral and distant forms of third-person narration still lean in the direction of the syntactical world of the point-of-view character. To try to get humour out of funny sayings when representing a character who isn't funny (his or her situation is, but he or she isn't) would be wrong. It would feel wrong, and therefore, would not be funny.

So, write in the voice of, and from the knowledge and culture of, the fictional character, as you would in any other kind of fiction, is the best advice.

✦ ✦ ✦ Politically Correct Humour

And now for a word about political correctness, which various people have represented as the death of humour, its strangulation at the source. This subject has run its course, but I bring it up here because of how well it illuminates a question of great importance to writers of humour. That is: *who can be the butt of whose humour?*

It is glib to stand behind Lenny Bruce and contend that humour must be free. Political correctness came about because groups in society were being damaged, ridiculed, and held back by disparaging stereotypes and jokes. Political correctness didn't come about because these things occurred (they always had); it came about because the stereotyped groups decided not to take it anymore.

There are two kinds of political incorrectness. One is deliberate and the other allegedly innocent. Deliberate political incorrectness is synonymous with black humour. It goes in search of taboos, the things the society is most tender about and embarrassed by, and it flouts those taboos deliberately. Black humour is not nice; it is not meant to be. It is often cruel, the crueler the better. Bad taste is good. This is how we got *Challenger* jokes instantly after the blowing up of the space shuttle, Woody Allen jokes after he married his daughter by adoption, dumb blond jokes in the age of feminism, and so on.

To detect black humour, just ask if it flouts a taboo. If it does, it is.

Why we like it is an interesting question. Some say that to laugh at death takes some of the fear of death away. But that doesn't account for all our fondness for black humour, not by any means. It is funny for the same reason that you can always get a child of three to laugh by saying "pee pee." The adult version is to laugh if a joke is unkind; if it flouts taboo.

There is different humour for different audiences, different venues, different times of day. Black humour used to be private humour (between friends, between people at work). Then it became late-night public humour. It is now moving out of those niches into the world at large, into prime time. The more liberal the society, the more quickly this movement happens.

The second kind of politically incorrect humour is the kind that proclaims itself innocent of the charge. The person behind it claims that he has honourable intentions, is being misunderstood, is the victim of society's straight lacedness. (And I am using the pronoun *he* deliberately because the person who does this, in my experience, is always male.)

This is far different than black humour. The innocent one does not understand that he is flouting a taboo—he doesn't understand the taboo.

We have all heard the innocent's defences:

- I really like (Natives, women, Jews, and so on); that's why I joke about them.
- I hear (Natives, women, Jews, and so on) making these jokes about themselves all the time.
- Some of my best friends are (Natives, Jews, women, and so on).

An understanding of this whole business of political correctness can be found in these statements of defence. The person who says these things assumes that friendship with or fondness for the people he jokes about entitles him to make the same jokes they do. Or he assumes that the fact that they joke about themselves entitles him to joke about them. And he's wrong. He should remember that he can make fun of his mother, but probably wouldn't stand for it if anyone else did.

In the age of PC, we are still entitled to make fun of ourselves, of our tribe, of our society—of any group, as long as we are part of it. If we make a claim to belong to a group and can't back it up, the people who are in it will let us know.

Here's an example of what I'll call a chain of belongingness: the groups to which I belong and therefore can write humour about. I am a man. Okay. I am a writer. Okay. I am a farm boy. Okay (though if I were to start making fun of farmers, I would probably be told that I'm not a farmer anymore). I am an Albertan. Okay. I am a Canadian. Okay (unless I use my nationality as an excuse to make fun of subgroups of Canadians, such as Maritimers and Natives, to which I do not belong).

My collection of short stories, *Working Without A Laugh Track*, is about sex and health in the late-twentieth century. It pokes fun at the highly medical approach my generation of adults took to conception, the prevention of conception, reproduction, and to the end of reproductive capacity. These were all things that my parents' generation thought about very little, but that my generation thought about a lot. The group to which I was claiming membership when I satirized these things was the group of men and women who shared the experience.

Why exactly can we make fun of ourselves and our groups? Because there is an assumption of fondness, fairness, and sharing the sting of the joke. If you are part of what you satirize, you will likely be warmer and less cynical. If your humour happens to be that of self-loathing, expect your humour to be criticized; expect it to fail.

When I wrote my book *Teeth*, I was in one sense out of the group I was satirizing, because I am not a professional hockey player. But because I have always loved to play hockey and watch it, I could claim membership in the greater group that is obsessed with hockey. At the same time, that doesn't stop me from noticing many things about professional hockey, or even the game of hockey, that are excessive and verge on insane. If I had hated hockey, never watched it, and tried to satirize it, the whole venture would have failed—because I would have got it wrong. It is hard to satirize that which you do not know, inside and out.

The other group you can innocently satirize is the powerful. Here, you don't have to belong. In fact, if you do belong, it doesn't work. If you think of how vicious comedians and columnists are on TV and on radio, and wonder how they get away with it, the usual answer is that they are picking on the powerful. People make the joke that the only thing left to joke about is white heterosexual males, and there is some truth to that. It is somewhat true because that group still is, statistically, an advantaged group in our society. Big business, government officials, the mega-rich, the big unions, rich athletes, rich athletes' agents, owners of sports franchises, movie stars—who says we're badly restricted in our comedic opportunities in the age of political correctness?

My belief is that you can still make fun of most of the people you always could make fun of. You can kick people when they're up, never when they're down. What really is wrong with that as a rule?

✦ ✦ ✦ Your Process

- Imagine two eccentric fictional protagonists. Write a paragraph about each one just to make sure that you know them well.

- Imagine two normal fictional protagonists. Write a paragraph about each one, again so that you demonstrate your knowledge of them.

- Imagine a situation for each eccentric protagonist in which he or she would be rendered a misfit.

- Imagine a situation for each normal protagonist that would turn him or her into a misfit (for example, the honest, respected employee who is stuck with a charge of theft).

- Choose the character and situation that seems most promising to you and write a monologue from that character's point of view (first-person or third-person).

... 12

Self-Editing Your Fiction

BEING BETTER THAN YOU ARE

This is the first of two chapters on editing. The first deals with major structural editing and the most basic trouble-shooting questions. The chapter following will look at fine tuning: the smaller more final stage of editing and polishing, after you are satisfied that the story is working.

Often when we talk about revision, we pretend that there are two distinct stages in the writing process. In the first, you produce a first draft; you create the story for the first time, beginning to end. Then you move to subsequent drafts, each one making the story better through editing until it's finished. Let's call that editing or revision.

It's not as simple as that. Every writer has a writing and editing process that is to some extent unique. Editing can begin the instant the first sentence is born. Some writers would write the beginning ten times until they were sure they had launched successfully. Others wouldn't care what the first sentence was but would write on as fast as can be, thinking they would fix it all later. Others will fall in love with their words and not want to change anything. And so on and on.

Once, when editing an anthology of commissioned new writings, I wrote into the structure of the project an editor's first assessment and comments after the first draft. This wasn't well thought out on my part. This was a book for which I had commissioned proven professional writers, many of whom probably hadn't had anyone look at their first drafts since they were in school. But because the process involved a government agency and a means of releasing funds, I felt I had to do it—and so was afforded a rare peek at what first drafts were for this group of seasoned writers.

Some writers amazed me by how finished their first drafts were. What was left to do? A nip, a tuck, a little polish. Other writers amazed me because their first drafts were so rough, so sketchy, so thrown together. Some of these looked hopeless to me, like something that might best be abandoned, but at least I had the sense in these cases to hold my tongue. I did go on fearing that the result might be failure, which was heartbreaking, considering these were writers of the first rank, some of the best I'd ever read.

Then I got their final drafts. Indeed, the people with the polished first drafts hadn't changed much. Often, I had to go back to the first draft and compare to find the changes at all. As for the people I feared could not possibly make a good story out of their sketchy first drafts, all of them had produced a work up to their usual high standard.

This was one of those humbling experiences, of which life serves up so many. I realized I didn't know a thing about editing. I knew what it was for me, but I didn't know what it was for anyone else. I had made that disastrous assumption (that fiction writers of all people should never make) that others worked as I did, because after all, wasn't that the most sensible way?

✦ ✦ ✦ Two Types of Writers/Self-Editors

As you might have suspected from the warm-up anecdote, I have discovered that writers can be classified into two groups: those who write complete and polished first drafts, and those who write crude and sketchy first drafts. But that's not the generalization yet.

What I have found to be generally true is that writers of the first type (polished first drafts) tend to be people who dislike editing, who don't do a lot of it, and who have strong beliefs about the superior qualities of the first draft. The second type (crude first drafts) tend to be the reverse. They often don't like writing the first draft and can't wait to get it out of the way so they can move on to the more serious and enjoyable business of editing it, improving it, turning it into what they want.

In other words, how writers view editing obeys the principle by which children usually judge an endeavour. If they're naturally good at it, they like it; if they're naturally not good at it, they don't like it.

To some extent what we are talking about here is the writer's nature. And, no, I wouldn't attempt to turn one kind of writer into the other. But I do have certain beliefs about how the first kind of writer, the swift writer of quality first drafts, can hit a ceiling in his or her development if skill at self-editing is not developed. I have those feelings because that's the kind of writer I am—or, hopefully, the kind of writer I used to be.

I started writing young, had a small success with an early novel at the age of twenty-two, then had a long drought in which I could not seem to create anything of quality. I was on a long plateau. Then finally, my work started to improve again.

I wrote my first novel at weird speed. I remember writing ten thousand words in a single day. It was during my post-university year of bumming around Europe, and I was on a train at the time, from the south of England to the north of Scotland. The whole novel was only sixty thousand words in its final form.

What this experience gave me was a certainty that this was what writing was, this headlong charge, this gust of words, this feeling that the story was telling itself and I was merely recording it. And what a wonderful feeling! I sought to recapture the feeling, to relive it, by writing many novels; blasting through first drafts, touching them up, sending them off, having them rejected. I was addicted to first-draft writing and possessed in equal measure an aversion to editing. Editing seemed too much like work, too much like school. I associated it with authority.

When asked to speak about my theory of writing in those days, I would talk about the beauty of the first draft, how there was a rhythm in it that had to be respected. Revision could be chopping into that rhythm, committing surgery on something you probably didn't even understand. I blamed unwarranted revision for much of the woodenness and stiltedness I saw in the published work I read and didn't like.

Do I repent of saying these things? Not entirely.

What I still believe about the first draft, especially in the case of someone who is able to write it quickly, fluently, is that it is not respected enough. Sometimes writers do chop it up too soon, thinking that's the mature thing to do. By doing so, they may neglect its best qualities, which often are the rhythm, the propulsion, the lyrical fluency, that can come from headlong writing. What makes a writer write fast can make readers read fast, which is generally a good reader response.

But it is very hard to improve as a writer unless you learn to self-edit. My first drafts might have been good, but they weren't good enough, and they were never going to be any better until I developed a facility for self-editing.

What converted me into a self-editor was watching other writers develop, writers of the second type, the ones who liked editing more than first-draft writing. Again and again, I saw and admired the density of their final work, the complexity, and I began to appreciate that they were achieving those values through layer upon layer of editing. If a first draft has rhythm and a headlong propulsion, it is also often thin. To thicken it, you need to edit.

To use the candle-making metaphor again, you keep dipping it. It keeps getting thicker, gaining body, becoming more complete.

Where all this led was to an epiphany about writing I would like to hand on:

Writing is one of the few human endeavours where it is possible to be better than you are.

If you are a golfer, you are as good as you are today. But what if, instead of going out and hitting the ball a hundred times, sometimes well, sometimes badly, you were able to put together your best drives, best irons, best puts, into a single game? You still might not be Tiger Woods, but that one game might be of professional quality.

In writing, through editing, you can do exactly that. If you edit in a disciplined way, for as long as it takes, you can keep improving your story until it is as good as you can make it. How wonderfully unlike life itself, where we are stuck with our opening performances.

Another apt metaphor is the difference between a band that can give a terrific onstage performance, and the kind whose top quality is achieved only in the studio. Often you hear about this difference as criticism of the studio band because it can't go on the road or doesn't go on the road well. As writers, we don't go on the road. We might be called on to read aloud to audiences from our finished products, but we don't have to sit down and write them in public as part of our craft. Our process can remain as secret as we want it to be. If we show anything less than our best to the world, that's our choice, not anything forced upon us.

When I understood this fact, I understood why compulsive self-editors were so fervent. I understood why their work was always improving while mine seemed to stay at the same level. It gave me a motive to become a self-editor. And I did.

✦ ✦ ✦ Time and Distance

Before moving into a discussion of the craft of editing, I want to speak to the matter of how you can make yourself see and hear your writing anew, as a stimulus to the next set of edits. That is, how can you get sufficient distance from the writing so you are not hearing it exactly as you did when writing it? If you've written it to your satisfaction, and you hear it exactly that way on rereading, your instinct will be to say: it is fine; it is perfect; it is as good as I can make it.

The most obvious way of achieving distance from your writing is to set it aside. Leave it alone long enough so that, when you pick it up again, you are reading with a reader voice, not the writer voice that created it. That may be obvious, but it is also often impractical, given the conditions under which people work. Some people's minds retain the sound of their writing for a long time. They may have the words so well ingested, so well memorized, that they won't be able to hear it anew for months.

Another impracticality of letting time do its work is that, as writers, we often struggle to set aside precious, too-brief periods of time to write. If you've taken time off from your life and work to hide and write, it is by definition precious time, and who wants to sit back during that time, twiddling thumbs over the keyboard, letting time pass so you can hear with the ear of a reader?

So let's move on to other, more practical possibilities. The next most-obvious system is to give your work to somebody to read. Given an intelligent reading of the work, sensitive, and positively disposed to what you're trying to accomplish, this method can be useful. It can show you your work in ways you hadn't thought of. It can confirm strengths and weaknesses you half-understood. This is the principle on which many creative-writing programs work, including The Banff Centre Writing Studios, where I have worked as a faculty member for fiction. At Banff, writers and editors are paired to work on the writer's manuscript. Advice is given, which the writer is free to take or not. The writers at Banff are good and so are the editors, and it works well.

But seeking the second opinion of a reader as a way of editing your works-in-progress can go seriously wrong, it is only fair to warn you. If the reader is a friend or relative, there is always the problem of their saying it is wonderful, which pleases the ego in the moment but does little good beyond that. Or not being an expert, the reader may give you a bad reading or bad advice. (Experts can also give bad advice.)

Another problem I have with seeking the help of others in the process of editing is implied in the title of this chapter. The chapter aspires to help you become a self-editor of your fiction, which is what we all need to learn. Some writers replace learning to self-edit with a sequence of outside editing experiences. This too can be a matter of private process, and I shouldn't be too presumptuous about criticizing it, but I know it has held many writers back. What they have done is *outsource* the editing stage of their writing. They never learn to edit for themselves and perhaps never intend to.

To achieve the necessary distance for editing, other than by setting the work aside or going to an outside editor, you might try any or all of the following:

* Have a friend read your work to you aloud. (Don't tell the poor person that he or she is reading it wrong. Just try to hear it as one reader is reading it.)
* Work on another piece of writing, until you are hearing it in your head rather than the piece you want to edit.
* Read a different book; if it is a book with which you engage deeply, it should break the chain between your writing voice and reading voice, allowing you to hear your writing anew.
* When reading aloud or when reading somebody else's work, subvocalize— that is, hear the words aloud in your head—whether you normally do this

or not, as it will help you to get a different sound than your writing into your head between editing phases.

✦ ✦ ✦ Structural Edits (Major Edits)

There is an obvious difference between editing your work by the line and word, and making big structural changes (changes to plot or character). It probably makes sense, as it does in house construction, to move from the big jobs to the finishing touches, so that you don't waste time perfecting that which is going to change.

If you have been successful at getting distance and can make an assessment of your story as a whole, good questions to ask are:

- Where do the points of greatest interest happen in the story?
- Are there flat spots, where you believe readers might be bored?
- Does anything of real significance happen to the protagonist?
- How long is the story before the first significant event?
- How long is the story after the final turning point; after the event toward which the story has always been moving?
- Did the story seem to be writing itself?
- Could you, after writing the first draft, write a monologue in the voice of the main character on any topic?
- Do readers have a problem engaging with the story?
- Is the story confusing for readers?
- Do readers frequently disengage from the story?
- Does the story seem emotionally flat?
- Does the plot work, but the effect seem blunted?

✦ ✦ ✦ Troubleshooting Your Fiction

The remainder of the chapter is divided up into problems you might detect in your story after a first draft is complete. I aspire to provide a troubleshooting guide—like that in the owner's manual for an appliance or a car, where you are told what this groan might mean or how that failure to perform might have been caused.

✦ ✦ ✦ Soft Spots in the Story:
Does Your Character Think Too Much?

Another of Merna Summer's metaphors for fiction-writing is that it's like pulling on a rope, keeping the rope taut, all the way through. Logically then, something to do at the major revision stage is to look for places where the rope has gone slack. These soft spots or slack places are places where readers will disengage through boredom, where if they're asked to describe their feeling, they might say, "I was reading but not paying attention."

Sometimes the problem of dullness or flat spots has to do with the difference between action and introspection, the rhythm that exists between the two. We are often told to write in scenes, to have characters doing things and involved in conversations rather than just reporting what was done and said. It's good advice, but another piece of good advice is never to interrupt a scene during its action or conversation for any length of time, for any reason, including introspection.

Introspection needs to be motivated. If your character is having an argument, or running from a foe, or trying to climb from the neighbouring balcony because she's locked in her only key, it is not a good time to have an interior monologue about fear of heights and how it developed when Uncle Art took her onto the roof at the age of four. There is no logical space for it. Besides breaking up the action and disrupting the readers' suspension of disbelief (turning them into disbelievers, in fact), you are also destroying the fictional scene's reality. If time can stop while your character has a big think, then the story is not real.

And why would you want to do that? Sometimes, as writers, we forget what is exciting about the story we tell. If we know we are at an exciting point, why interrupt it? It's not as if we can sell advertising in the forced interval.

There is a place for introspection in fiction, of course. Fiction can hardly ever do without some inner reflections, some thinking time. But that place is seldom inside an active scene or one filled with conversation. Just ask yourself when *you* think. I think in the car when I'm driving. I think when I'm alone. I think when I'm taking a walk or riding a bike. I think while I'm doing some gardening or household task that is routine and doesn't occupy my mind. If I had a character thinking during an intense, interactive scene, I would want it to signify something: that the character is aloof to the other character; that the character is self-absorbed to an almost clinical degree.

Have your characters do their thinking in the quiet times, the natural lulls, and it will create a rhythm of action and reflection through the story that is satisfying for readers, realistic, and not frustrating.

Introspection can be the culprit in a story's flat spots in another way. Introspections often go on too long. While they do, the present action of the story is suspended and goes cold. Define the present moment of your story (the horizon on which the real action will occur), and have as a rule of thumb the idea that you should never leave it, for any reason, long enough that it grows cold for readers. It's the same thing exactly with flashbacks. Writers are often told that flashbacks are bad, but I don't think they're told often enough why. For starters, flashbacks are not intrinsically bad. But they can be bad for the story if they take you away from the present story long enough that that story is forgotten or loses its heat.

✦ ✦ ✦ Are the High Points and the Highest Point of the Story in the Right Place?

A good story often proceeds in waves or successive peaks, which, if you're a mathematical or visual sort, you may be able to see as some kind of graphic illustration of readers' level of interest as they read through. I like to imagine this illustration as a diagnostic method when dealing with my own or other people's fiction, because it clarifies for me what is going on. If I feel dissatisfied with a piece of fiction, it may well be because the highest point was near the beginning or in the middle, and the story never got to those heights again. Though it is not the eleventh commandment that a story should climb in interest, beginning to end, or should rise in the sense of coming to larger and larger peaks of interest, it does make sense that this rhythm would be satisfying for a reader. Graphing the interest level may prove a good way for you to analyze what you have written, to find out why it isn't as satisfying as you want it to be.

If a story has too long a preamble (introduction of theme or characters, and so on) before the first thing of significance occurs, that could create a flat spot. If the story goes off on a long tangent in the middle, however interesting, and lets the main storyline go cold, that could create a flat spot in the middle. If the story does not go anywhere, if nothing of significance happens in it, that creates a flat spot at the end. If the graph is descending rather than ascending as you move toward its finish, that sounds like a problem structure to me.

The end is where you can least afford to be flat. How often I've read a story or novel that thrilled me for the first half, and then didn't go anywhere. Like many a promising oil well, it watered out. For all the excitement of the first halves, these are not the stories and books I remember with most fondness. I will never read them again or recommend them to anyone.

✦ ✦ ✦ Does Something of Significance Happen?

The idea that there needs to be a significant happening might draw some argument, because once again it seems to privilege the story in which the *Titanic* sinks over the story in which the sewing machine breaks and it's the final straw. Significant doesn't mean big and gaudy. It might even be possible to invent a character who survived the *Titanic*, but for whom the event lacked significance. It remains a strong rule that something should happen and that it should be significant. When analyzing a story for its problems, asking that question can be the key to isolating why you're left feeling unsatisfied.

✦ ✦ ✦ Did the Story Ever Seem to Be Writing Itself?

The feeling that the story is writing itself is an indicator that the characters have come to life: they have their opinions and values, and choose their path at every crossroads, or fail to choose well for their own reasons. A quality of deadness can often be traced back to the characters' not having come alive yet. They may only be stick figures that you are manipulating. If you have manipulated them through a fine plot, the story can seem successful but dead at the same time. It went somewhere; something interesting happened; what happened should have been significant. If it doesn't feel significant, if the story still feels dead, then look to character.

Another way of testing the vitality of your characters is to write a monologue from the character's point of view. (This you will recognize as an assignment question from the characterization chapter.) If after writing a draft, you can't easily write such a monologue, then character is probably where you need to concentrate to get the story to come to life.

✦ ✦ ✦ Does the Story End in the Right Place?

How to end the story, with which deft touch, is something for which there is no rule. One sensible thing you can ask, if the ending doesn't seem to be working, is if the story has gone on too long. The distance from the story's climax to the end should be brief.

Going on too long is often only a sentence or two. There is a magic spot to leave the story that allows you to end on a key word or phrase that relates back to the start or to the title or to the meaning of the story. Try and find it and not overrun it.

Something else that may cause a story to overrun its best ending has to do with introducing new material too far into the story. There comes a point, somewhere in the story's last half, where nothing new (new characters, new subplots, new information) should be introduced. By then, you should be narrowing in on your ending. The desire to throw in something new is often a kind of bailing out, a desperation move. Resist that desire and finish the story you are writing. If you have introduced something new late in the story, you have to deal with it; you have to resolve it. This dealing and resolving often pushes the story longer than its natural end.

✦ ✦ ✦ Does the Story Begin in the Right Place?

My usual advice about revising a story beginning is that you should wait until you've done everything else. How can you know how a story should begin until you know how it has ended? The same is true of titling. Usually, the story ending and the story beginning should have some resonance between them, some interplay of ideas or words, so it makes sense to revise them both last.

The rules of thumb about beginnings are: don't go on too long before the first significant event of the story; don't bog down in exposition that can be eliminated or scattered farther along; ensure that the reader is informed and not confused by your beginning; and start in the tone that will dominate the story (that is, don't start with burlesque hilarity when the story is tragic or vice versa.) There should be some strong indication in the beginning of what kind of story it is: comedy, tragedy, farce.

✦ ✦ ✦ Does the Story Feel Emotionally Flat?

Remember the exercise of writing about a favourite room or your back-yard or somebody, then writing it again flavoured with this or that mood? Often in workshops, this exercise liberates writers. Something happens that hasn't been happening for them. The second writing of the paragraph is almost always much better than the first. It is motivated, engaged, detailed, in a way that the first was not. It may not have occurred to them that writing always differs according to the emotion it is charged with.

The importance of this awareness to the editing stage is that writers frequently forget the mood that should imbue a moment in their story. They get carried away writing, and they may write a lovely passage that doesn't work for some reason. To give a crude example, let's consider a story in which a character dies. The main character is affected by the death. The deceased was his best friend, his worst enemy, a loved one. If the next scene is not imbued with the emotion the death evoked, there will be a falseness to that moment, an emotional irrationality, an emotional deadness.

✦ ✦ ✦ Is the Reader Having Trouble Engaging with the Story?

This is a recap from previous chapters. The problem of readers failing to engage with fiction is often caused by not allowing them to see and hear the story. If you write in scenes, this problem shouldn't arise. If you don't write in scenes, what you're doing is standing between readers and the story, blocking the view. Then, instead of getting out of the way, you aspire to be helpful by telling them what they are not seeing or hearing. Try to get out of the way.

Lack of engagement can also be the result of a poor opening. If readers don't understand the story well enough at the outset to engage with it, you may never get them back.

Too much introspection relative to action, especially introspection illogically inserted into active scenes, will prevent or break engagement with the story.

✦ ✦ ✦ Does Your Reader Disengage Too Easily and Too Often from the Story?

Once readers are engaged with the story, the ideal is to keep them that way. To put this goal in less manipulative and more accurate language, you aspire to allow them to stay that way. If the story is having problems in this area, the spell of the narrative will break too easily and often, forcing the reader to frequently re-engage.

The problem may be that you are switching point of view within scenes. For more detail, return to Chapter 7 on point of view in fiction.

Another cause might be too many transitions: too many jumps in time, or in place, each one forcing disengagement and requiring re-engagement by the reader. If you make a time transition ("A week later") or place transition ("Back at Tom's house") to a new scene, and hardly anything happens before the next time or place transition, you are forcing too many disengagements, and you're probably frustrating your readers. Ask yourself if smaller scenes couldn't simply be summed up in a transitional narrative paragraph. For example:

> *Over the next two weeks, Tom saw Julie three times, once at a ball game, once at the mall, once while he was walking his dog and she was returning from work. They never spoke and made eye contact only in the sense of pretending not to.*

Frequent disengagement from your story can also be caused by a reader's confusion. Is the story hard to follow? Are you being too clever, too mysterious, and leaving your reader behind?

Is there a lack of clarity across transitions? That is, on the far side of a transition, are readers wondering where they are? If there's a plot reason for wanting them to feel that way, fine. But if that's not your intention, fix it up. Make the landing more secure. I'm a believer in simplicity on the far side of transitions. If the scene before the transition featured a big fight between lovers, I prefer an opening that tells me quickly when and where I am relative to that scene. For example: *A week after the fight, Sam returned to Elaine's apartment with a bouquet of spring flowers.*

An example of a post-transition sentence that doesn't allow a secure landing is:

> *Sam put the bouquet of flowers in the sink. He turned to her and said, "I thought about it and I don't think it's important." She was tucking a strand of hair behind her ear.*

Readers probably won't know if they're still in the same scene, or if Sam went straight out after the fight and bought flowers and now he's back. If as the scene goes on readers still don't know, you've got a bad kind of confusion that is preventing engagement with the scene. All the writer had to do was say "Two weeks later," but writers often feel it's a sin to be so simple, a sin against art. To my mind, confusing readers, who are not engaged with the scene and therefore not getting the juice I've put into the scene, is a greater sin against art than being obvious.

Editing is often done by instinct. Something doesn't feel right; you change it. Instinctual editing works best at the level of the line and word. It is harder to detect the bigger, broader problems, the structural ones, in this gut way. I hope this chapter will help you. Even if the particular performance problem of your fiction isn't listed in the troubleshooting guide, I hope the argument in favour of becoming a stronger self-editor is convincing.

✦ ✦ ✦ Your Process

- By now, you have finished a first draft of one of your short-story ideas. Begin a structural edit by asking each of the questions in the list on page 169.

- Does your story have dialogue? If not, it might be an indication that you're not writing in scenes and are telling the story instead. Find a place in the story where you have reported the dialogue (that is, where the narrator sums up what was said) and force yourself to write out the dialogue. In this sequence, stick to action and words spoken by the characters. Don't allow the narration to interpret what is said. See if this approach enlivens the scene.

- Find a place in your first draft that feels emotionally flat. Ask yourself: What is the point-of-view character's emotion in this scene? Rewrite the scene with this emotion in mind.

- Go through the draft and highlight all the places where your character is thinking, and the story is recording these thoughts. Look at the overall balance between the highlighted text and the remaining text. Are there places where the introspection is interrupting scenes in a way that couldn't happen in reality?

- Draw a graph of the story that shows the high points and their relative power. The horizontal axis of the graph registers the pages of the story. The vertical axis measures readers' interest/excitement.

...13

Fine Tuning

Having challenged the structure and asked all the tough questions about whether the story is working in major ways, there comes a time to fine-tune. As said at the end of the previous chapter, this stage is often done instinctually. It is not necessary that we be able to explain why one wording is better than another; it is sufficient that we feel it is so and act on that feeling. But here are a variety of things you can do at the fine-tuning stage: things your instincts may or may not have already guided you to do.

✦ ✦ ✦ Trimming

I have often heard writers say the words, "It's as tight as I can make it. There's not a single excess word." I have heard myself say it too. It's amazing how untrue it always is. When freelancing articles for magazines, you are often asked to shorten a piece for reasons that have nothing to do with whether the work is good. It will have to do with whether the piece fits the page, or if at the last minute an advertiser has asked (and paid) to have its ad enlarged. The editor will say, "It needs to be 110 words shorter," and off you go.

Luckily, there has never been a real-life equivalent to this experience in my fiction writing, but the experience in forced pruning did serve a purpose that relates to my fiction: it proved that you can always tighten more; there are always words that are not doing anything, not even for rhythm. The work usually benefits from their absence. On occasion with my fiction, I have acted as though a magazine-type editor was standing over me, saying, "Cut this by 10%." And I have done so, just because I know it can be done and the result will be stronger.

I have already proclaimed my dread of the adverb. Perhaps I should explain why I hate it, so that I can advise you to hunt them down and at least ask what they're doing for the piece. I dislike adverbs because they are after-the-fact. The verb instructs me to run or hide or wake up or seize an object, and then along comes an adverb to tell me to run quickly, hide immediately, wake up instantly, seize the object fiercely. But as a reader, I've already visualized the action. What am I supposed to do? Un-visualize it, go back, visualize it again with the appropriate adverbial twist? That makes no sense. If adverbs are put ahead of what they modify, like adjectives, they make more sense—which of course you can do, though not often.

The second reason I dislike adverbs is because they all end in "ly." When you're trying to build a complex sound, and a rhythm that suits the action, a part of speech that always has the same sound, which rhymes with all other adverbs, imposes a gaudy separate sound and rhythm that tends to overpower anything more subtle.

That's my rant. If you agree, one of the things you can do in the name of trimming is hunt down and remove excess adverbs.

While you're at it, look for the word "very." It is not really a modifier. It does not add impact and stress to the word it tries to modify. It is stuffing, and it can always come out. It improves the relationship of the adjective and noun to take "very" away.

"He was very tall."
"He was tall."

"*The woman she was talking to was very thin.*"
"*The woman she was talking to was thin.*"

For my money, the second of these pairs is stronger than the first. The tall-ness and the thinness have more impact when not modified by "very."

"Very" is one of several words that pad a writer's prose to no purpose. Look for other false modifiers like "just," "much," "a bit," and "too." These all fall under the heading of overqualification. You're trying to be exact, so instead of saying that someone had lunch, you say they had "a bit of lunch," because they didn't eat much. The difference matters or it doesn't, and usually it doesn't. Looking for places where you're trying to be too fine is another way of trimming.

Overqualification can also be a sign of hesitancy. If the tendency is justified by the character through whose point of view you are writing, that's fine. But watch for places where, like a bureaucrat, you are playing it safe.

✦ ✦ ✦ Cliché Hunting

In the final stages of editing, it never hurts to see if you are using clichés for no better reason than that they came to mind. That's why they are clichés, because for reasons of overuse in the society, they do leap to mind whenever a context they suit presents itself. We write instinctively, and so what leaps to mind tends to go on the page. If you want to write without clichés, sooner or later, they have to be found and replaced.

The only justification for clichés is if they represent a character culturally, or if the use of clichés is part of the character. Then it makes sense to allow them to stay.

✦ ✦ ✦ Dialogue

When writing quickly, a writer sometimes confuses the voice of one character for another, or has all the characters talking alike. To test if a char-acter's lines sound like they come from that character, a good exercise (easy in the age of the computer) is to cut and paste that character's dialogue together, and read it as a disjointed monologue. This will sometimes show you the line that doesn't sound like the character. Also, by comparing these cut-and-paste blocks of dialogue, you can compare one character's vocalizations to another's. You can see more obviously if they are the same. Especially in places where the spell of culture is powerful, people do tend to talk similarly, and it would be wrong to individuate them beyond their cultural bonds. That too can be discovered by putting the lines together and comparing.

You probably remember my earlier rant about not replacing *he said* and *she said* in your dialogue with anything more colourful (choked, spluttered, sang, grieved). Now would be a good time to check. Often you can do away with the *he said* and *she said* too. If the conversation is between two people, and you have identified the speakers at the start of the conversation, and they are taking turns talking, there is no reason to identify them again and again. It's padding. Some feel the rhythm calls out for it anyway. I seldom use it if I don't have to. (A case where you do have to identify the speaker is when the same person speaks twice in a row.)

✦ ✦ ✦ Diction and Syntax

Diction and syntax were defined in an earlier chapter. You may have heard the term *syntax shift*, which means a sudden change within a text from one type of syntax to another. A *diction shift* would be a change in the kinds of words you are using.

In fiction, the choice of diction and syntax is often governed by the point-of-view character. The narration will tend to lean in the direction of that character's diction and syntax even if the point of view is third person. Everyone has a world of syntax and diction that is influenced by their place in the world, their class, their generation, their interests, and the writer will stay within that world when it comes to diction and syntax. If the writer strays too far outside it, there will be a diction shift or a syntax fault. To give an exaggerated example, if your character prides himself in his good grammar, the narration that represents him wouldn't normally contain grammatical errors. Finding these shifts and faults is another job for the fine-tune stage of editing. The most glaring of these, the faults that the reader is most likely to read as faults, are those found in dialogue.

✦ ✦ ✦ Details

In various places in this book, I have stressed the need for specific, apt, curious, startling, telltale details. The general word as compared to the specific word lacks impact. The general word or phrase lacks the ability to put an image in readers' minds. This interferes with or weakens readers' engagement.

A logical thing to do during fine tuning is to go back over and see if you have any general descriptions and words left in the work that could be improved on with detail and specific words. If the problem is that you haven't been to the place you are describing for a long time, or at all, why not go there and take notes? (If it's somewhere you can't go to, maybe you can pull up some pictures of it on the Internet.) If it is an object, find the object and look at it. If it's historical or foreign, do one last bit of specific research.

Recently, I was writing a historical fiction about 1880s Montana. I had, in my early research, come up with some interesting guns. I finally chose a Colt Dragoon for my main character's weapon. In the fine-tuning stage, I realized I knew what the gun was for and why stockmen liked it, but I didn't know what it looked like. I went on the Internet, found in five minutes an Internet gun vendor who had a photograph of a Colt Dragoon. I discovered that it had an engraved battle scene on the revolving bullet chamber. The insertion of this detail made all the difference.

The recommendation is to go through and check all the details. Find the ones that are poor and improve them. If more research is necessary, it's never too late to make the story better.

✦ ✦ ✦ Title, First Line, and Ending

If you are not in love with what you have in these three categories, take the time to try again. Often, rather than being satisfied, we simply give up. We tried to think up something better and nothing came. This doesn't mean you can't have another go and be successful. Often, with little hope of success, I have forced myself to do a formal, specific exercise toward improving some specific item. Often, it's the title. I'm not a gifted titler. I'm much better at recognizing good titles when I see them, so what I will do is go through a story line by line, phrase by phrase, trying out every single thing as a title. That is, I say them aloud in my mind. "Something Better." "Nothing Came." "Hope of Success."

Often the right title is there. If not, I will force myself to write twenty titles. Just when it seems most hopeless, a better one is found.

✦ ✦ ✦ Consistency

The mistakes that are most embarrassing when someone else finds them are, for example, when your characters' hair and eyes change colour halfway through the story. I've even had mine change name. It makes it look like you're not paying attention and don't much care. What in fact happens is that writers get so used to seeing the words the way they are, they stop thinking about what they mean. The most obvious error in the world will not be visible to them. But if you think that physical details like hair and eye colour, names, and places of origin are the types of details where you tend to make mistakes, force yourself to check them. Make a key of them as you read through that you can check against.

This kind of mistake also denotes, of course, a failure to picture fictional characters in your head, because if you have a strong picture, you won't change it by accident. Likewise, if you say that a man's from Vermont on page one, and he's from Medicine Hat on page ten, you're not ingesting your characters' biographies. You're writing superficially, as if it didn't change anything or matter if someone was from Medicine Hat as opposed to Vermont.

✦ ✦ ✦ Bumps

If I have tended in the writing of a work to hear it only in my head, something to do at a late stage is read it aloud. What is often gained from this exercise is the discovery of lines that are hard to read. I'm used to reading them in my head. I never fail there to read them as intended. But reading aloud might trick me to read it more as another would. Of course, if you have someone around who will read it aloud for you, that's even better, though many of us have a tendency to get defensive and blame the volunteer for reading our work incorrectly.

✦ ✦ ✦ Your Process

- If you haven't already applied all of the above fine-tuning exercises to your almost completed story, please do.

- Pick out a book you admire and apply the fine-tuning questions to it. See if you can find any diction shifts, in dialogue or narration, and any syntax changes. See what makes the dialogue specific to one speaker or another.

- If you have chosen a quiet, pedestrian, informative first sentence, try one last time to choose another line that still suits the story and its point of view, but has more allure, surprise, or mystery about it.

- Are you happy with your title? If not, try the exercises proposed in the titling section. Look through the whole story phrase by phrase. Try each phrase or combination of words as a title, and see what you come up with.

- Take an anthology of short stories, and see if any of the titles there would work for your story. Once you understand why, try to come up with a title that relates to the story in the same way: different words, same concept.

- When you've finished your polish, remove another sixty words. Make sure you do this exercise on a hard copy so that you don't lose what you remove.

- When you've finished the above, remove another fifty words. Again only do this with a hard copy. Use a different pen colour for the last thirty. (If you feel you've gone too far and that you were carving at the heart of the living tree, put the words back, and call your story complete.)

...14

Writing Fiction as a Profession

REJECTION, PUBLICATION, FELLOWSHIP

Those serious enough to complete a story or novel usually want to see it published. Writing is a means of communication. It implies a reader. But I want to begin this chapter on the business of writing fiction with a cautionary tale about what can happen when the goal of publication gets ahead of the desire to write.

I started writing fiction as a teenager and finished my first novel *Lonesome Hero* when I was twenty. The novel was published by Macmillan of Canada when I was twenty-two. For about a wonderful month, I experienced literary success. In hindsight, it was a modest success, but I had no standard of comparison. The novel was kindly reviewed around the country. I did my first radio, TV, and newspaper interviews. I launched, I signed, I won an award; I went home.

Brief as it was, I craved to repeat this experience. I sat down and churned out stories and novels, dreaming of another published book. But except for the odd short-story publication, and an annoying habit of finishing second in contests, nothing much would happen. I often felt lousy about my writing. Because writing was so central to my life, I felt lousy most of the time. Everything about my first book seemed like a fluke. I wondered if I had done something to my brain in the interval since writing it.

It took me five years of suffering before I first wondered if I shouldn't stop writing fiction. It had become painful, and because no one cared except me, I could stop at any time and relieve the pain. So, I did. I allowed myself to stop writing fiction, at least for a while, but possibly forever.

I don't remember how long the stoppage lasted. The length of time doesn't matter. I stopped until I began to feel a new pain, a withdrawal and then home-sickness for a favourite activity lost. I began to understand how much I liked writing fiction. It was failure that I didn't like.

I began to write fiction again, with much less concern about publication. Not submitting things proved to be easy. Some of the innocent joy that brought me to writing in the first place returned.

I look at what I've written above and see that some of it is exaggerated. I did not entirely lose the desire to publish. As I said at the top of the chapter, that desire is probably rooted in and implied by the act itself. It may be impossible and pointless to try to stifle it. But when I stopped writing fiction, the desire to write well gained weight while the desire to publish went on a diet. On my personal writing scale, there was balance. There was sanity.

As tends to be the case, that was also about the time that I started enjoying success again: a few short-story publications in literary quarterlies and anthologies; a couple of book publications with small presses. To the ambitious beginner, this might not sound like enough, but it is what most serious writers of fiction have as a career. Good presses were publishing me for the right reasons. Readers were telling me they liked what I was doing.

Because my literary goals had become less short term, one of the effects of this change of values was that I began a more ambitious novel project, a book that I knew would take a long time to finish. In 1985, I wrote a commissioned non-fiction book about the western Canadian fur trade for Parks Canada: a guide book to the Rocky Mountain House National Historic Park. The novel I proceeded to write was on that subject, based on the fiction-worthy material found during the research.

That novel, begun in 1985, wasn't completed until 2000, the year it was published by Douglas & McIntyre under the title *The Trade*. I wrote many other things in those fifteen years, including two short-story collections, another novel, and numerous videos, but I would always come back to the manuscript of *The Trade*, spending more and more hard-won, expensive time on more and more drafts.

When I thought of this effort in career terms, I would feel the old rise of panic. I was in no way sure the world was interested in this book, or that a publisher could be found for it. It seemed possible that it would wind up in a drawer, in which case I would have committed career suicide, given the amount of my time, years of it, that I had devoted. When I thought about it as a novel, however, I remained fascinated by the process of finding the story inside it, of learning to tell that story.

Luckily, the ending to this story is happy. *The Trade* was published by Douglas & McIntyre. It was nominated for the 2000 Giller Prize. It proceeded to sell better in Canada than anyone had expected it to. It won three awards in Alberta. In short, it produced all the publicity and opportunity that I had so craved back in my twenties. Best of all, I was able to sit down and write a new novel, not with any certainty of commercial or critical success, but with confidence that I knew a little more about how to write a novel and was unlikely to take another fifteen years to complete it.

I wanted to tell this story at the head of this chapter about the business of writing fiction because such a story would have been useful to me at the beginning of my career. Back then, I was hearing lots of stories about the romantic and inebriate excesses of my literary heroes, but there was almost nothing about their self-doubt and failure. It gave me the impression that they never had self-doubt or failure, which increased my feelings of doubt and failure as I groped around for a voice and a form for my fiction.

In the last few years, one of the pleasures of my writing life has been to edit fiction and to direct a writing studio at the Banff Centre for the Arts. It is an opportunity to work with writers of all ages and backgrounds who have had some success, but are still in the early stages of their careers. They are all talented and accomplished. At some time in every studio, I find myself listening to a conversation about the agonies of rejection. They often discuss the meaning of the hierarchy of rejection slips and letters from *The Atlantic Monthly*. First of all, there's the basic two-line rejection slip, the standard one, which everyone gets. But then there's the better two-paragraph rejection, with a squiggle of initials at the bottom. The real excitement is if anyone has received an actual letter from an actual person at the magazine, saying that, while the story exhibited talent, it wasn't powerful enough. At this, the other writers enviously ooh and aah.

To some extent this is healthy. Everybody needs a bunch of rejections just to be able to partake vividly in conversations like these. It's probably essential to the development of tribalism in each mini-generation of writers. But every once in a while, I detect real pain, the real fear of people who are afraid that these rejections mean they are no good and that success will forever elude them. Where I've thought it appropriate, I've taken such people aside and suggested that the one sure way to prevent the pain of rejection is to not send anything out for a while. These are good writers, improving with every story. They will, in time, reap some rewards. When they do, they will probably look back at their former anxiety about failure and rejection as wasted pain. I'm not telling them to cease their pursuit of publication. That would be silly. What I am saying is that, during a period of improvement as a writer, why not take a break from the wars of the marketplace and let yourself improve in peace? Later, when some new plateau has been reached, try the market again. If there is justice in the world, your batting average should have improved in the interval.

Now to the meat of the chapter. Having been a writer for a long time means that I have met a lot of aspiring writers. I know what questions they ask and which of these questions recur most often. The rest of the chapter is made up of these questions and my answers.

✦ ✦ ✦ What Should a Fiction Manuscript Look Like?

It might sound facetious, but the answer is *perfect.* In the age of the reasonably priced computer and the high-quality printer, there is no reason not to produce a perfect manuscript every time. Believe me when I say that editors at periodicals and publishing houses expect it.

I know that some writers will be angry to imagine an editor turning thumbs down on them because their manuscript was messy, and I have to say that the writers in this case are failing to imagine what the editor's life is like. A publishing house might have hundreds of manuscripts around the place at any one time. They stand in piles, waiting to be read. What the editor charged with reading them would like is for the ones he or she will not enjoy or recommend to jump out and declare themselves now, and to volunteer to get back home under their own steam. Then the editor could cozy down with the small remainder.

But the editor has to go through everything, and how hard is it to imagine that he or she will be prejudiced in favour of those that look clean and professional, as opposed to those that have creased edges, nubbed corners, and handwritten additions and corrections? The same response is likely for obvious spelling and grammatical errors.

It is no different for an editor at a literary quarterly. I was this creature once. Not nearly often enough, I would head down to the office, which was far out of my way. I would unlock the office door and find a dishearteningly tall stack of brown envelopes. I would haul them home and start pawing through them. The ones that were difficult to read because of poor presentation or typing, or bad machinery, probably went to the rejected pile faster than most.

There are a few things that I can confidently tell you never to do in terms of your manuscript.

- Do not try to enhance the look of your manuscript beyond its being a stack of white pages. The stories in the fancy jackets, the ones with illustrated title pages, the ones tied in ribbons, the ones on handmade paper, the ones on coloured paper, do not look more enticing to an editor; they look childish and unprofessional.
- A short-story or novel manuscript should be double-spaced, one side only, on white paper.
- The manuscript should have a separate title page on which the title, number of words, and your name as author are centred. Somewhere at the bottom, add your mailing address, phone number, and e-mail address.
- No one should have to be told this, but bitter experience tells me to tell you to number your pages. I number in the top-right corner because that's what the reader can most easily see. I like it when a writer puts either a last name or a fragment of the title with the page number in the header so that, if things get mixed up, they can easily be sorted out again.

- Do not include explanatory footnotes within the text. Do not ever try to communicate with the reader of the manuscript within the manuscript. ("What I'm getting at here ..." "This event actually occurred ...")
- Don't staple or fasten the pages together with anything more than a paper clip. In the case of a staple, the first thing editors will do is try to get the staple out. If they get it up between their fingernail and their finger, your chances of a sympathetic reading are history.

✦ ✦ ✦ Is a Manuscript Written on a Typewriter Still Acceptable?

Yes, unless it looks sloppy (for example, because of a dead ribbon or uneven key strokes). But I have to wonder why a writer would cling to a typewriter when a computer can do the job so much better. I have seen the documentary films about great writers, the ones who are still plunking away on the Underwood portable, on which they wrote this or that famous novel. I understand that loyalty, that clinging to familiarity. But I would suggest that the easiest way to emulate these great writers is not to emulate them at the technological level; emulate their dedication and ability as writers instead.

Computers are great. Computers and word-processing software and printers are as if the whole genius of the world was devoted to the problem of how to make writing easier for writers. I can say without any doubt that the computer has made the business of writing a hundred or a thousand times easier for me.

The computer has also made me a better self-editor. In the old days of typewriters, we would use up bottles of white stuff, painting out our mistakes and typing new words into the holes. Rather than retype a whole page, we would look for a solution to the problem that would fit into the existing whited-out hole. If an edit would require us to retype an entire page, or several pages, we would often work on our own minds instead, seeing if we couldn't learn to accept it the way it was.

Technological resistance might be charming in a veteran writer. In a writer younger in years or in an earlier career stage, technological resistance looks like unwillingness to adapt. That signals difficulty, obstinacy. A writer who resists technology might turn out to be a writer who resists editing with the same iron will, which is fine if you are a superior self-editor, not so fine if you need the advice.

✦ ✦ ✦ What Is a Query and When Do You Use One?

A query is a letter combined with a sample of the manuscript that you send to determine if a publisher is interested in seeing the rest of the manuscript. This applies to book-length manuscripts and not to individual short stories. With short stories, you send the whole manuscript with a cover letter.

The tradition with novels and short-story collections is that you query first. Some publishers will not even accept a query. This is where you need one of those books like *Writer's Market* that contains lists of publishers with thumbnail descriptions of what they do and don't publish and how they want to be approached. If they say "no unsolicited manuscripts, please," they mean that they want you to query first. If they say "no unagented manuscripts," they mean that too. They want to be approached not by you but by your agent. How you get an agent is another topic.

Before I get to the query for a book-length manuscript, let's talk about the cover letter that you send with a short-story manuscript. Brevity is the key here. Tell them what the title of the story is and anything relevant about yourself. I often do no more than this: *Enclosed is my short story "Destitute." The story is 3,200 words. Attached to this page is a list of my publications.* If "Destitute" was about the life of a cowboy, and I was a cowboy, I might add a sentence to that effect. My belief about cover letters is: Why would they care to know a lot about me? What is the point, when the short story is attached, of explaining what the short story is about?

A couple of things *not* to do: Do not tell the editor that this work is your first short story. I don't understand why writers do this, but they do. It's like a dog lying on its back in a posture that says "I'm defenceless. Don't kick me."

Some might argue the opposite, but I don't see the point of explaining why you wrote the story either. Again, why would an editor-in-a-hurry, who doesn't know you, care? The truth is that most of the things that authors add to their cover letters, in hopes that they will make the editor read the story more sympathetically, stimulate the opposite response. Some might say, "I'm trying to make sure that the editor really does read it." Well, if the editor is the kind who throws things aside without reading them, any special pleading in the cover letter will ensure it happens. A good editor, whose job it is to read your story, will read it, or will read it until he or she is sure that it isn't working or isn't otherwise right.

You can include a list of your publications and awards within the cover letter or attach it (as I do) on a separate sheet. I don't think one approach is better than the other. If you have no previous publications, do not tell the editor that. Just avoid the subject. Don't start explaining why you don't have publications yet, or how you're going about trying to get them. Don't tell the editor about your near misses with other, more important periodicals. The editor of a literary quarterly probably believes his or her quarterly is the most important publication in the western world.

The query that you send out to a publishing company consists of a letter and a sample from your novel or short-story collection. Again, be brief. The reason the company wants to be queried is that editors and publishers want to spare themselves as much reading as possible. It makes no sense to send a big query.

The most important thing in the query letter is a brief synopsis of the novel or short-story collection. This is the hardest writing there is: an art in itself. If I could hire somebody to do it for me who could do it well, I would. Writers far too often bang one off and don't put a lot of thought or analysis or rewriting into it. What you should remember most is that you are both telling and selling your story. If the synopsis isn't interesting, you're doomed. A lot of writers try to thoroughly explain their book. Almost inevitably the result is boring. I think writers do this out of some Calvinist sense of honesty: *I must give an honest and complete account.* But you don't, and that's not what the editor wants. The editor wants to be wowed or brought to his or her knees laughing or crying. At least, the editor wants to be powerfully intrigued. Maybe you can overdo this, but the more grievous and common sin is to underdo it.

Brevity is all-important in a synopsis. If you can boil it down to half a page, great! Another important fact is that the synopsis should have the same selling qualities as the novel. If it is a funny novel, the synopsis should make the editor laugh. If it is tragic, the synopsis should be tragic. And so on.

Otherwise, take the same approach as in the cover letter with a story. Why explain why you wrote it? Why tell your life story? Why mention your lack of success thus far?

The query is an important piece of writing because, inevitably, the editor is trying to figure out whether the book is good and if you are good. Obviously, it needs to be well written. It needs to excite the editor. As for you, the editor is probably most interested in your sanity. If you sound straight-up, normal, and capable of making sense in a short number of words, the editor will go on to the writing sample without prejudice.

With the writing sample, brevity is still important. I would never send more than twenty pages, and I might, if I had the right piece from the novel, send as little as ten. Again, don't fall into the trap of being thorough, or wanting to send some part that the editor will fully understand in the context of the novel, or trying to supply the part most likely to convey the novel. *Send the best part.* The most riveting part. The part that makes you laugh or cry. You want a strong reaction from a tired editor. Period. Anything else will see your query rejected most of the time.

A synopsis of a short-story collection is harder still. If it's a linked collection, say that, and synopsize the overall plot. If the stories aren't linked, is there some clear and compelling theme that unites them? If the stories are the twelve that you have completed so far in your life, and are not connected by anything else, don't say that. Synopsize a couple of the stories and list the subject matter of any others that have obvious selling appeal. Again, you don't have to be thorough and complete. You don't have to list the titles. You don't have to give the subject of each and every story.

As for the work sample, why not send the best story, provided it isn't mammoth? Or if the mammoth story is the one you think will sell the book best, send an excerpt from it, stopping at a major moment of suspense or at the height of a good scene.

✦ ✦ ✦ How Do I Get My Novel or Story Back?

In the case of a short story, the only way to get your story back is to enclose a self-addressed stamped envelope (SASE). Periodical publishers cannot or will not send back your stories at their expense. If there is no SASE, they throw it away. Put on your covering letter, at the bottom after your signature, "SASE enclosed."

Just for the record, when the computer came along and postage rates went up, I quit sending SASEs. I instructed editors that, if they weren't interested, to please destroy the copy. The cost of receiving it back was not worth it. I would include a letter-sized envelope, addressed and stamped, for their reply.

In the case of a query to a publishing company, I would again send an SASE. As above, my preference would be for the company to discard the sample chapter or pages, and send me only a reply, and for this I would supply the letter-sized SASE.

In the case of a full manuscript, the tradition is not to supply the return postage. Some publishers are on record as saying they will not send the manuscript back, if rejected. Some still do send it back at their expense, if you queried and if they asked to see it. If you really, really want it back, you could send a money order for return postage.

✦ ✦ ✦ How Do I Choose the Publisher or Periodical to Submit My Work To?

First off, let me say that this decision should be researched. To pick periodical or book publishers and send to them without knowing what they do is a careless use of time and money.

In the case of periodicals, back issues of literary periodicals are often hard to get your hands on. Some of the bigger bookstores and newsagents will stock a few. Otherwise, go to the library and read back issues there. If neither of the above is possible for you, get a list of periodicals from a recent edition of a writers' market book (found in a library or bought in a bookstore) and write to them, asking to buy back issues.

However you go about it, find and read the periodicals. Find out which ones publish work you like. Chances are this is the kind of work you write, and these are the periodicals most likely to publish you. By reading periodicals, you can with a modest amount of detective acumen figure out basic things about what they buy. Does the periodical ever publish a story written in the first-person point of view, for example? If that's what you write and the periodical never publishes it, they are unlikely to make an exception. Sometimes you will note a marked preference for stories set in other countries or involving characters from various ethnic backgrounds. Depending on what you write, that could be a good or a bad thing. Experimental or mainstream? High tone or vernacular? Hard-nosed or non-violent? These are the sorts of things you can figure out.

Another thing to do is look at who edits fiction for the periodical. You find this information on the masthead. Not always, but often, these fiction editors are writers. Why not run their name through the Internet, or through a library index of periodicals, and see if you can find any books or stories by them? This is not a science, but it seems to me that a writer whose writing you like might be a better person to send your fiction to than a writer whose work you don't like. Besides, wouldn't it be more pleasing to send your fiction to someone you admire?

As for novels and collections of short stories, I take more or less the same approach. Go back to the books you love, especially the recently written and published ones, and remind yourself who published them. If you don't own the books, go to the bookstore or library and do some research. Take notes. By studying who publishes whom and what, you'll start to see patterns. You'll start to understand the market the way a good agent does. Often writers will go to the big how-to-write-and-publish marketing books and read the thumbnail descriptions of the various publishers they find there. There's nothing wrong with this, but reading that a publisher "takes mainstream fiction, including historical, but no romances or science fiction" can't possibly tell you as much as knowing that they publish this or that author whose work you know. As mentioned before, what the writers' market tomes can tell you is how the publisher insists on being approached: by query, by agent, and so on.

If you are using the annual books with the lists of publishers and periodicals, make sure you're using a current one. Periodicals and book publishers move addresses, go out of business, and change staff. Using old lists is a bad gamble.

✦ ✦ ✦　How Do I Get an Agent?

The process for getting an agent is pretty much exactly the same as that for seeking a publisher. Agents are not interested in marketing individual short stories, so if that's the position you are in as a writer, forget about agents for the present. If you have a book-length manuscript and you have decided you want to try to get an agent to represent it to the marketplace, then you begin by getting an up-to-date list of agents. Most writers organizations have this kind of list. Some of the writers' market books also do. Beware of agents who want a "reading fee." Some of these agents are ethical and some not. Some make their living off reading fees and hardly ever find a publishing contract for anyone. To figure out which is which, you might again go to writers organizations and ask what they know about this or that agent. While you're at it, why not simply join a writers organization or two, so that you are helping to pay for the services you require? Most writers organizations have newsletters filled with this type of information.

Once you have a list of agents, how do you choose? In Canada, there is a periodical called *Quill & Quire*, which is a trade magazine about the book industry. In it, there is a section devoted to recent sales by agents to publishers. This is a great way to find out which agents are most active and successful and which writers are represented by which agents. The approach I advocate is the same one I suggested for choosing a publisher or a periodical to send your manuscript to. Choose the agent who represents the writers most like you or whom you most admire. Start there.

Have you any hope of getting that agent?

It's not going to be easy. If it were, everyone would have a great agent. There aren't enough to go around. They're not charities. I've heard it said that first-time authors can never get agents, and while that might have been true at one time, it's not an iron-clad truth now. The fact is that the present fiction market is interested in new authors, and publishers are paying some amazing advances to the chosen ones. If the fiction publishers are looking for new authors, it follows that fiction agents are trying to find them first.

The first-time authors who have the most luck getting agents are, according to my limited observation, the ones who:

+ have a few publications in respected periodicals,
+ have won a respected manuscript competition,
+ have completed a degree or two in creative writing at a respected university, and
+ are being vouched for by a well-known writer.

The same list of attributes might represent you well to a publisher.

The way to approach an agent is to find his or her address and send a query: the same kind of query that you would send to publishers, with the same need to convince them that the book is hot and you are a reasonable individual. When approaching an agent, talk more about your preparation for being a writer. Have you studied creative writing at a university? Do you have previous publications and awards? Are there known writers with whom you have studied or who have been your mentor who are willing to vouch for you? To enclose a letter of recommendation from a well-known writer would certainly help.

Again, keep the manuscript sample short, and select the piece most likely to excite interest.

✦ ✦ ✦ What Is a Literary Periodical and Is There Any Sense Sending Them Stuff?

A literary periodical is usually a quarterly (four times a year). It is usually perfect bound, like a book. Literary periodicals vary according to what they publish, but most will publish a few short stories and a few poems or suites of poems in each issue. They often combine the literature with good design and/or art photographs or drawings. They may be affiliated with a university or college, or they may exist outside of any institution. They are usually started out of a love of literature by a community of writers, editors, and readers for the further-ance of the literary endeavour in their city or region. They are financed partly through subscription, but their following is usually small enough that their real survival depends on government grants or private donations. And for that reason, they do not pay a great deal. Some pay only in free copies.

Though you should feel free to send your stuff to the *New Yorker* and *The Atlantic Monthly*, most Canadian careers in fiction begin in literary quarterlies like *The Fiddlehead, Grain, Malahat Review, Descant, Prism International,* and *Dandelion.* (These examples are all Canadian.) Publication here is important because the standard tends to be high. The readership may be small but within it are many writers and editors, people who, if they are impressed enough with you, might select your story for an anthology they are editing or might come looking for you to see if you have a book. It's usually not a straight-line connec-tion like that, but it is one major part of how many literary reputations are slowly constructed.

An excellent example of how this works in Canada is the Journey Prize, a $10,000 award to a short story published in Canada in a recognized literary quarterly during the previous year. The list of contestants results from the editors of the various quarterlies sending in the story they deem their best. Out of that list, judges choose a short list, which is published in *The Journey Prize*

Anthology, alongside this year's winner. Mark Anthony Jarman has been selected for *The Journey Prize Anthology* several times, and partly for that reason has one of the strongest reputations in Canada for the writing of short fiction. Yann Martel is a former winner of the Journey Prize. In 2001, his novel was nominated for a Governor General's Award.

✦ ✦ ✦ Is It a Good Thing to Enter Competitions?

Yes. There is an argument afoot about whether contests and awards make up too much of the literary landscape, but an apprentice writer need not be concerned about that. Often writing competitions are judged by well-known writers. Sometimes, there is a preliminary screening before the celebrity panel sees the finalists; sometimes, they read them all. At any rate, it is an opportunity to be assessed relative to your peers by people who know what they are about. Winning such an award goes on your resumé and can help you in any number of ways.

Some literary quarterlies stage competitions with an entry fee, usually a fee that happens to be the cost of a year's subscription, which you get, win or lose. Some find this unethical, and I'm not one of them. As with most things in the writing business, it is your uncoerced choice whether to spend your nickel or not. If it seems unfair, don't do it. It wouldn't hold me back because, chances are, I'd already be feeling guilty if I wasn't a subscriber. The point they might be making is: Why should we support you if you don't support us? I have always found that argument compelling.

When you enter a contest, don't put your name on each page of the manuscript or on the title page. Or you might provide two title pages, one with your name and contact information and one with only the title. Why? Because most of these contests are judged "blind," without the judges knowing who has written the manuscript. If your name is all over it, they might disqualify you. Failing that, they have to go over the manuscript with a black marker, obliterating your name wherever it appears.

✦ ✦ ✦ How Seriously Should I Take Rejections?

If you use the scattergun approach to submitting for publication (mailing stories to magazines you've never seen), rejection may very well mean nothing. It might mean that you have sent a story about death from alcoholism to a magazine sustained by liquor ads. It might mean that you sent three thousand words of gritty, hyper-realism about junkies to a Christian family magazine.

If you are tailoring your approach to the so-called marketplace carefully, something may be learned from rejection. There always is the possibility that the story came close to being chosen (though because that is good news, the editors will usually take pleasure in telling you). There is also the possibility that yours was the fifty-third story the editor read that day, and it was two a.m. and he or she was no longer concentrating. Or maybe your story about a runaway teenager describing why her parents drove her to it has landed on the desk of an editor whose daughter has just run away. You'll never know.

Anything can happen, and that is why one or two rejections shouldn't be regarded as telling the whole tale. You need to be honest with yourself. You need to develop the ability to compare your work with the work published in the market you have chosen and to tell yourself whether yours meets the standard. You'll always hear about the story that was published on its thirty-third try, but I would take the hint and go back to the story long before that.

Not winning a competition should never be taken too seriously. There are as a rule more entrants in a competition than submissions to a periodical. This implies that the judges are under a heavier reading load. There is a famous tale of a Toronto poet who decided to test the preliminary screeners of a major Canadian literary competition. He typed a number of famous stories by famous writers into ordinary, modern-looking manuscripts. He ascribed them to made-up authors and submitted them from post-office box addresses. When I say famous authors, I mean people like Mark Twain and Italo Calvino. Not one of the stories he submitted was selected to go to the final round of judging, and I have never heard it said that the screeners sniffed out his plot.

I don't know how this happened, but apparently it did. As for whether it means that good stories are routinely overlooked at periodicals and in contests, I doubt it. When I called for submissions for a short-story anthology in 1986, I stated that unpublished work was preferred but that published work would be considered. I was hoping to have a book substantially made up of never-before-seen material, because I thought that would be more exciting to readers. Invariably, when a submission read well, and looked like a contender, I would discover at the end or in the covering letter (which I tended to read last) that the piece had already been published or broadcast, or had won or placed in a competition. This experience led me to believe that the publication and award machinery was operating at top efficiency and missing little.

✦ ✦ ✦ Is It a Good Idea to Take a Degree in Creative Writing?

There was a time when I would have said it didn't matter. I still believe (having been self-taught) that it isn't essential. But I do think that pursuing a degree is at this time a strong approach to learning the craft and business of writing fiction. To put it in its most crass form, I believe the agents and publishers are shopping at the best creative-writing departments for the next big talent, the next hit book. The University of British Columbia's Master's in Creative Writing has a grad list that looks like an encyclopedia of up-and-coming Canadian talent, which either proves that the degree is providing strong teaching or that the degree is a powerful magnet for talent.

While knowing there are wonderful creative-writing instructors out there, I have observed how much students teach one another. Because of their extreme desire to achieve and make a career in fiction, they often know more about agents, competitions, publishers, editors, and periodicals than their professors. As the approach to creative writing is often to workshop, the students are doing much of the work of analysis and editing for one another, so a strong set of fellow students is of key importance.

Perhaps to state the obvious, not all creative-writing departments are equal. I can't see much sense in submitting to one that isn't good. If you have the mobility to choose a creative-writing program (and the talent and portfolio to get in), I would advise you to carefully assess the people teaching. Most are writers. Read their books. If you admire what a writer/mentor writes, it's a good first step toward knowing if you want to take a degree from the institution at which the person teaches. The reverse is also true. If you don't share the mentor's aesthetic when it comes to fiction, I think it would be nearly impossible to learn from him or her.

Others don't have the mobility to choose, other than to choose to go to the local university or college, or not to go at all. Here it is harder to say no, because it might mean doing nothing. But I have seen writers slowed down, if not damaged, by advice that was not good advice for them. Good mentors look at you and what you are trying to write, and if it is a viable literary form, they work with you to make it the best novel of the kind that you can write. Bad mentors try to turn you into a version of themselves. This can, I believe, be subconscious, a kind of feedback loop where mentors applaud that which reminds them of themselves, and criticize that which they find too different.

But my advice should also be taken with a grain of salt. I did not come up this way. The opportunities to do so when I was in my twenties were few. Now they seem to be everywhere. There were certainly satisfactions in going it alone, but as a professor of creative writing once told me, the benefit of the degree (given a good relationship with good mentors) is a speeding up of what might happen anyway. This rang true. Going solo almost certainly cost me time. If the process could have been sped up, that would have been a good thing.

There are also non-university opportunities out there for the learning of the fiction craft. The writing studios at The Banff Centre are a good example in Canada. There is one entry-level studio (which inevitably attracts higher-level writers who want the opportunity). Then there are two long studios (one that consists of a five-week residency at Banff and one where the residency is two weeks, followed by twenty weeks of mentorship on-line). These studios attract great writers who go on to accomplish great things. The method in the long studios is to team up each writer with one faculty mentor. The writers are asked to work only on their own manuscripts. There is no workshopping. The interaction among the participants is warm and strong, a compressed and perhaps even more generous version of the longer-term bonding that takes place in a university program.

Other non-university opportunities include workshops in craft, writer-in-residencies that are open to the public (often hosted by libraries or colleges), evening non-credit writing workshops, and private writing groups. In every case, they are good if they are good for you. If you are making gains through them, you have made a good choice.

✦ ✦ ✦ Are Writing Organizations Worth Belonging To?

I warn you, I'm loaded for bear on this question. The need most writers have to know other writers can be served in many ways, and this chapter has already mentioned several. As a writer who was self-taught, I found that my hunger for a peer group of writers could not be fed in a classroom. The Writers' Union of Canada and the Writers Guild of Alberta became that peer group. For a long time, my relationship to those organizations was entirely social. Later, I became interested in what they did, which was to lobby levels of government on issues affecting the working lives of writers, to seek funding for the creation of opportunities and services for writers, and to police the fair play of publishers. Eventually, I would serve those organizations by belonging to committees and serving on boards and executives.

Even if your social and informational needs are being met elsewhere, I believe in belonging to writers organizations. For over a decade, The Writers' Union of Canada (TWUC) struggled to achieve a payment to writers for the library use of their books. A few other countries had this kind of compensation in place, and TWUC believed Canada should too. Led by writers Matt Cohen and Andreas Schroeder, TWUC finally talked the Canadian government into it. The federal government funded the creation of the Public Lending Right, from whose commission I receive a welcome cheque every spring.

The Writers Guild of Alberta (WGA) urged the Alberta government to create an arm's-length foundation to which writers organizations and writers could apply for juried grants. Again, it was a struggle, and again the WGA got what they asked for. That foundation was the single most powerful innovation in the public support of writing in my home province, and without the WGA, it would not have happened.

Both TWUC and the WGA can count on my being a member for as long as I have funds to pay my dues.

Few things disturb me more than writers saying, "Why should I pay to belong? For a crummy newsletter?" They never seem to understand, or simply don't care, that thousands of hours of other writers' time were given up to create structures they now use without a thought.

Besides, the crummy newsletter probably contains information you need to know.

✦ ✦ ✦ Is It Possible to Have a Career in Fiction?

Possible, yes. A living earned entirely from the proceeds of my fiction is something I have not yet achieved. Few people I know have. If you made a list of the twenty writers in your country you believe make their living from fiction, you might be surprised by their biographies. If they are currently making their living that way, chances are they weren't until recently. Many successful writers are or were university professors or other kinds of teachers. Others, like myself, work in other branches of the writing trade (videos, films, ad copy, radio, commissioned non-fiction books, newspapers, and magazines).

Occasionally I'm asked whether I would advise someone to try to make a career in writing, and I dodge it every time. Eel my way out, and run. Fiction writing is more of a calling than a lot of careers. Romantic as it might sound, you have to have an intense, sustained, driven desire to do it, the "fire in the belly" we're always hearing about. A phrase that a friend and I came up with once describes what a fiction career is: "It's a big job, and nobody has to do it." If you're trying to make sense out of a writing career, I don't think it can be done. The same amount of energy and time poured into understanding the stock market would certainly pay off much better.

However, writing is an enjoyable way to make a living. You do, as they say, work your own hours. You do choose your subject and make all the decisions relative to your writing project. There is the simple transporting experience of being within a world you have created. That feeling is hard to beat.

Whether or not you make an all-out attempt at a writing career will be determined by the strength of your desire: the same thing that brought you to writing in the first place. Those who must try will try, and I can only wish you the best of luck. I have been a writer for thirty years, and it is a career choice I have regretted only on occasion—usually the occasion of not getting a publication or writing job that I was counting on. I have tried a few times to be something else, most recently a locations person in the movies. Nothing drove me back to writing quite as dramatically as that!

✦ ✦ ✦ Your Process

The final assignment is to take the stories you have thought up, written, and rewritten and try to market them.

- Go to a university, college, or city library, and ask for a list of magazines and periodicals that publish short fiction. Librarians don't get asked nearly enough questions. They like answering them. In my town, the librarian takes you to books or organizational newsletters that list short-fiction markets. Use the list to help you find what the library holds. Gather back issues and head for a table.

- Some of these publications will be magazines, and some will be literary quarterlies. Separate them into two piles on that basis.

- Begin reading short stories. At the head of a page in your notebook, make note of the periodical's name and the date. Then under that heading, make notes on each story. Record what it's about and how it's told: point of view, type of protagonist, traditional realism or experimental, formal or vernacular, violent or not, action-packed or psychological. Don't necessarily use my list. Devise your own according to what you see in the stories and how you tend to classify fiction. Don't stop at reading one issue of each periodical. Read a few and then you can test your assumptions and generalizations about their choice of fiction. Don't forget to record in your notes the mailing address and the name of the editor (and the fiction editor's name if there is one).

- Choose a magazine or periodical that seems to suit your story the best. Write a cover letter to the person who edits fiction for the periodical. Only name the person if you saw his or her name in the most current issue. Otherwise, address the letter to the fiction editor (that is, "Dear Fiction Editor:").

- The big step. Photocopy your story unless you are confident in your computer and back-up disk system. Don't send your only copy, however you define only copy. Then prepare the SASE. Mail off your package, and see what happens. If you're sending to a literary periodical, don't expect fast results. Expect to wait months. This delay may seem all wrong to you. It may be hard to wait. But that is simply how long it takes.

Afterword

At the end of many books about writing I have read, usually the ones that are trying to sell you something besides the book, you are told that hard work and dedication toward your writing will always pay off handsomely. You will defy the odds and make a go at it—more than a go, a proper living, maybe even fabulous wealth.

I can't do it.

I am willing to say that the opportunities in writing have steadily and vastly improved through the thirty years that I've been doing it. I'm not talking about my own progress, which has been a roller coaster as opposed to continuous progress. But the conditions for writers have improved. There are more books of fiction published now than ever. The advances paid for them are generally better. There are more competitions, more grants, more benefactors, more places and ways to hone your craft, more honest agents (and dishonest ones, I guess), more writers organizations, better garrets, more writers to get to know, and more shoulders to cry on when it all seems hopeless.

The image of a writer is better too. The ink-stained hack isn't quite the popular cliché and automatic image that it used to be. When young people who don't know me ask what I do, and I say that I am a writer, they look like they assume I'm lying, or they perk up, smile, and get excited. *Writer* has a good connotation for them.

Writer has not always brought forth such respect. For a long time, writers were classed with dissidents and the people who might bomb your home. As for morality, writers had the same image problem as actresses and chorus girls. The fact that writers seem to be more respected members of society now is the best news I can offer to someone wanting to be one. It will do you more good than if I sang an evangelical song about how, with sufficient hard work and a good idea, you too could join the ranks of the rich and famous. The pay-for-publication publishers, the crooked reading-fee agents, the motivational speakers for hire will be happy to give you that kind of advice, but it never comes for free.

How will you know if you're a writer? The most reliable evidence is if you can't stop, if everything keeps turning to story in your head. Only then are you apt to keep at it long enough to get good enough to succeed.

About the Author

DON DENTON

FRED STENSON has written twelve books of fiction and non-fiction, and over 130 films and videos, during the course of a career that spans thirty years. His 2000 novel, *The Trade*, was nominated for the Giller Prize and long-listed for the Dublin IMPAC prize. It won the inaugural Grant MacEwan Author's Prize, and two Alberta novel awards. As a community and college writer-in-residence, and as a faculty member of several Banff Centre writing studios, he has served as a mentor and editor for many developing writers of fiction.

Contributing Authors

GREG HOLLINGSHEAD'S "The Dog in the Van" is included in his story collection *White Buick* (1992). Hollingshead's other story collections are *Famous Players* (1982) and *The Roaring Girl* (1995), which won the 1995 Governor General's Award. He has also published two novels, *Spin Dry* (1992) and *The Healer* (1998), which won the 1999 Writers' Trust Rogers Fiction Prize. His new novel, *Bedlam* is forthcoming in 2003. Hollingshead teaches literature and creative writing in the English Department at the University of Alberta. He is also director of Writing Programs at The Banff Centre.

DIANE SCHOEMPERLEN is the author of *Double Exposures* (1984), *Frogs and Other Stories* (1986), *Hockey Night in Canada* (1987), *In the Language of Love* (1994), *Our Lady of the Lost and Found* (2001), and *Forms of Devotion* (1998), which won the Governor General's Award in 1998. "Stranger Than Fiction" was originally published in her collection *The Man of My Dreams* (1990), which was shortlisted for both the Governor-General's Award and the Trillium Award. The story has been reprinted in her newest collection, *Red Plaid Shirt* (2002). Schoemperlen lives in Kingston, Ontario, with her son, Alexander.

EDNA ALFORD is the author of two collections of short fiction. She received the Gerald Lampert Memorial Award (co-winner) in 1981 and the Marian Engel Award for fiction in 1988. Her work has appeared in numerous anthologies including *The Oxford Collection of Canadian Short Stories* (1986), *Stories by Canadian Women* (1984), *Best Canadian Stories* (1985), and others. "Half-Past Eight" appears in her story collection, *A Sleepful of Dreams* published by Oolichan Books in 1981. Co-founder and co-editor of *Dandelion* magazine, and fiction editor of *Grain* magazine (1985-90), she has edited fiction and taught creative writing while continuing her own writing. She is has been faculty of The Banff Centre's Writing and Publishing programs for nine years, acting as associate director of the Writing Studio for the past five years, and is currently the director of Writing with Style.

RACHEL WYATT was for many years Program Director (Writing) at The Banff Centre. "Visitation" is included in her story collection *Mona Lisa Smiled a Little* (1999). Her plays include *Crackpot* (1995), *Knock Knock* (2000), and *For Love and Money*, which was produced by Alberta Theatre Projects in 2002. Wyatt's latest collection of short fiction is *The Last We Heard of Leonard* (2002). In July 2002, Rachel Wyatt was named Member of The Order of Canada.